Forty Days

Also by Ken Snyder

Cross Road: A Journey from Sex to Sanity

Forty Days

On the Mountaintop, Halfway Up,
and From Behind the Golden Calf

Ken Snyder

Foreword by Nate Larkin

RESOURCE *Publications* · Eugene, Oregon

FORTY DAYS

On the Mountaintop, Halfway Up, and From Behind the Golden Calf

Copyright © 2021 Ken Snyder. All rights reserved. Except for brief quotations in critical publications or reviews, no part of this book may be reproduced in any manner without prior written permission from the publisher. Write: Permissions, Wipf and Stock Publishers, 199 W. 8th Ave., Suite 3, Eugene, OR 97401.

Resource Publications
An Imprint of Wipf and Stock Publishers
199 W. 8th Ave., Suite 3
Eugene, OR 97401

www.wipfandstock.com

PAPERBACK ISBN: 978-1-6667-3378-5
HARDCOVER ISBN: 978-1-6667-2872-9
EBOOK ISBN: 978-1-6667-2873-6

NOVEMBER 11, 2021 11:21 AM

Scripture taken from the New King James Version®. Copyright © 1982 by Thomas Nelson. Used by permission. All rights reserved.

Scripture quotations marked CSB are taken from the Christian Standard Bible®, Copyright © 2017 by Holman Bible Publishers. Used by permission. Christian Standard Bible•, and CSB® are federally registered trademarks of Holman Bible Publishers.

The Twelve Steps are reprinted with permission of Alcoholics Anonymous World Services, Inc. ("A.A.W.S."). Permission to reprint the Twelve Steps does not mean that A.A.W.S. has reviewed or approved the contents of this publication, or that A.A. necessarily agrees with the views expressed herein. A.A. is a program of recovery from alcoholism only - use of the Twelve Steps in connection with programs and activities which are patterned after A.A., but which address other problems, or in any other non-A.A. context, does not imply otherwise.

Scripture quotations from the Authorized (King James) Version. Rights in the Authorized Version in the United Kingdom are vested in the Crown. Reproduced by permission of the Crown's patentee, Cambridge University Press.

For my wife Cassie, daughter of God and His greatest blessing to me

Contents

Foreword by Nate Larkin — xi

Preface — xiii

On the Mountaintop, Halfway Up, and From Behind the Golden Calf

Cowardice, Courage, and Stupidity — 3
"Was Jesus frowning or smiling at you?" — 6
"Look it up yourself." — 10
God Works in Mysterious Ways — 13
Cigars and Ink Pens — 16
Jesus is Lord Over Shreveport — 19
Angels Unawares — 21
"Be still . . ." — 24
Gambling (or let your "Yes" be "Yes", and your "No" be "No") — 27
The Color of All — 30

On the Mountain before Me

Joseph's Sentence and My Own Time as a Slave — 35
Blind Bart — 38
Moses, Me, and the Mount Rushmore of Anger Management — 41
"Let us also go . . ." — 44

On the Mountain with Me

Del and the Palm of God — 49
"Too-Hard-to-Handle Randall" — 53
Expectations and Pre-Determined Resentments — 56
Beautiful Tears — 59

Thoughtful and Measured Rants on Religion

Father Ron, the Non-Entity — 65
Pastor this or Pastor that, and How I Survived a Cult — 68
Splash Versus Sprinkle,
or the Difference between Relationship Versus Religion — 71
The vaccine — 74

Death on the Installment Plan

"Well, that went well." — 79
"Prickly" Marty and "Pre-Marty" — 82
"Cast the Devil Out" — 85
Car Wrecks and Kisses — 88
Two Steps — 91
Despising the Shame — 94

Faith and Other Adventures in Desperation

The Desire of our Heart and What to Desire — 99
Hope Images and Horsepower — 102
"Hey God, would you mind holding my coat for a 'sec'?" — 105
Manna and Better Days — 107
Post-It Notes and Other Trophies — 109
God the Golfing Partner (yes, God!) — 112

"I Know God Created Family But Good Grief..."

Breakdown in Aisle 8	119
Prisons of Presumption	122
Acceptance and Peace	125
My Son the Winner	128
Against the Wind	131
Loving God More than Family	134
Mame's Walls	137

An Imperfect Person But "Perfect Gift"

Bottled Tears	143
It Wasn't a Fair Fight	146
My Heroine on a Harley	149
Beating 50 Percent	152

A Couple More Random Rants: Dying and Maybe Someone who Should be Dead (?!)

Control Freaks and Controlled Freaks	157
Stage-Fright Stuttering and Miss Spry	159
On Death, Dying, and Dollars	162

Foreword

Pick a topic, any topic, and I'll come up with a personal story that relates to it in some way. I'm not unique, of course. You have stories too—thousands of them—because that's how we humans make sense of our lives. We are always constructing a narrative, telling ourselves a story that explains what's happening to us. And depending on how healthy we are, our stories can be either reliable or pure fiction.

During the decades I spent in active addiction I spun fantastical stories for myself and others. In some of those accounts I cast myself as a victim, mistreated and misunderstood, and therefore entitled to sympathy. In my darker moments, I painted myself as a villain, a blackhearted reprobate worthy only of disgust. (Those stories I kept to myself.) In most of the tales I created for public consumption I played the hero, drawing my sense of personal significance from the admiration I was able to win from the audience.

My recovery from addiction began in a church basement in 1998, in a 12-step meeting where I met a group of radical truth-tellers. These men were masterful storytellers, and the stories they told were the rawest, most honest, and most courageous I had ever heard. They spoke about their flaws and failures without shame or justification. They laughed—a lot—and they listened to each other without judgment. In the safety of their company, I eventually found the courage to begin reexamining the stories I had been telling myself and to edit them for accuracy. That's a process that is still underway.

I met Ken Snyder about 15 years ago, several years before he wrote *Cross Road: A Journey from Sex to Sanity*, and I liked him immediately. There is no one more winsome than a storyteller who is at peace with

Foreword

himself. Ken has a marvelous eye for detail, and he writes in a casual, conversational way. His faith is never far away, but he doesn't preach. Instead, he manages to talk about God and the Bible as naturally as you and I might bring up Walmart or the weather. So when I heard that Ken was putting together a collection of his stories for another book, I was eager to get my hands on a copy.

This book, *Forty Days*, is not something you'll want to read in a single sitting. There is so much to savor in these pages that you will probably find yourself reading it a piece at a time, finding fresh inspiration every time you pick it up. Whether he is telling a personal story or reflecting on one of the classic scenes from the Bible, Ken is always pointing us toward the light, inviting us to rethink the stories we have been telling ourselves. And here's what I know: the closer those stories are to the truth, the better it is for everyone.

Enjoy the book. Take your time. Listen for the wisdom in Ken's stories. Maybe, when you're finished, you can start re-writing your own.

Nate Larkin

Preface

More decades ago than I'm willing to admit, I wrote essays, devotionals—whatever you want to call them—for a small church's Sunday bulletins.

I dug them out with the idea of updating and compiling them into a book . . . and completely diverged from that plan. I tried with the old essays but launched into something entirely new each time. It came as a complete surprise. It's the most fun I've had as a writer because I never knew where the words were going to take me. I hesitate to invoke the name of C.S. Lewis as I, and practically all other writers, don't warrant mention in the same breath with him, but he said something I never forgot: "I am a writer, but the Holy Spirit is the author." I'm no C.S. Lewis, but I sure hope and pray that's the case with me in this book. I pray and believe the Holy Spirit took me to the new words.

Why write these essays and why should you read them? The answer lies in a question I asked a very talented wordsmith (as distinguished from "author") when he was going to write a book? He laughed and replied, "I don't have anything to say." I don't have anything to say either, at least in the way of instruction or wisdom. That's God's job. What I do have, I hope, is what *you* would say as you see your own experiences and life in mine. Ideally, what's in this collection of essays will open your eyes to what has been there all along. I would hope most of you would say, "Me too." "Wow, so that's what that was all about." "Hmm, I never thought of that, but yeah." Having a dysfunctional family isn't unique. Injustice and racism aren't things I alone see. The hypocrisy and hideousness, at times, of religion, is something most of us have seen (and if you haven't, you will). Many of

Preface

us have children and some of us, in retrospect, wonder why he had them, truthfully. Many of us have been members of borderline cults euphemistically called churches. And on and on.

There are also essays of love found. An encounter with a smart-aleck God. (Seriously.) Miracles you can drive both on and off a golf course (?). Friendships with a pedophile priest and a homeless man. The most eloquent and profound statement ever made since Jesus strode the earth. Life as a *controlled* freak. And more.

It's not my intention to make you laugh and cry within the same essay somewhere within this collection, but if you do, I'll know my mission was accomplished. I hope to not just touch your heart but have you look into it and learn something about faith, hope, loss, blessings, restoration, *you*.

Why the title? This will sound immodest, and a friend who spoke it probably missed the mark completely, but he told me that, like Moses, I was a *friend* of God. It's maybe the highest compliment I ever received. Being a child of his is one thing, being a friend is another. Becoming a friend, I believe, is asking God not what he can do for me today, but what can I do for him. Friends are there for each other. Can he do without me? Absolutely, but I ask to be a part of what he's doing, and he honors me by using me. I pray I am being a friend to him in helping others by writing these essays.

The title also comes from relating to Moses as a human being. He had rejection issues. He had some severe anger-management problems. (Can you say "murder"?) He had a speech impediment. He languished for a long time out of commission for use by God. He struggled with disorganization and was often overwhelmed. He knew disappointment and heartbreak. Except for the murder part, I've experienced all these things or struggle with the same issues.

Unlike Moses, however, my "mountaintops" were intermittent, sandwiched between times when I approached God half-heartedly, taking steps up the mountain with no real intention of getting to the top. I've also worshipped an idol—by definition, something between God and me—far longer than Aaron and the Hebrews worshipped a golden calf. I had an idol for decades.

To have seen God and experienced him at all is wondrous. He's happy for us to see him at work in our lives and experience him. Matter of fact, he sacrificed his only begotten son so that we could. I'm blessed. I pray this book will be a blessing to you as well.

Preface

One last thing: the title *Forty Days* has nothing to do with how many essays there are, and I'll save you the counting: there's forty-eight.

Blessings.

On the Mountaintop, Halfway Up, and From Behind the Golden Calf

"If life is a box of chocolates, beware of chocolate-covered rocks."
UNKNOWN

Cowardice, Courage, and Stupidity

The opposite of cowardice is not always bravery. Sometimes the opposite is stupid, as in sending a man to prison for five years who had all the potential in the world to kill me—the whistle-blower—afterward.

I was part of a ministry within a church that required reporting of any felony either past or ongoing. That's what I did. We advised persons we had to abide by this rule. The wife of this person I blew the whistle on disclosed an ongoing felony committed by her husband to women leaders in the same ministry of which I was a part.

It shouldn't have been a surprise that, when the wife spoke up, this was heavy lifting the women ministry leaders hadn't counted on. "Mum" was going to be the word, never mind that the disclosure was of something completely heinous and awful involving two adolescent girls, the daughters of the woman who brought the matter to light.

I'm not brave, and I won't admit to being stupid, at least not all the time. Let's just say I don't always think things through. In this particular case, I was simply angry—pissed off, to be more accurate—that someone could know two innocent young people were living through a life-scarring nightmare at the hands of someone, and a handful of badge-wearing church leaders wouldn't report it, letting fear lead them instead of leading. You signed on for the duty, do it, and if not, quit, and may I suggest you be deeply ashamed of yourself. I was borderline enraged that someone would not only overlook what had happened but also allow it to continue through inaction.

I didn't think twice (emphasis on the word "think") about what to do or that I could be the victim of a revenge murder. To go back to the brave-stupid continuum, let's just go with stupid. If you knew the perpetrator, you would think *really* stupid. Of the hundreds of people I had dealt with in ministry, this is the only person of whom I was wary. I'm all about kindness, but I instinctively gave this man a wide berth. Don't ask me why, it was just a feeling, an eerie quiet about this person. Nonetheless, I reported him to law enforcement authorities.

I didn't keep track of this person's parole or release, and I only gave it a passing thought that things might not be good for me when it happened. I do remember thinking (and here pops up "stupid," perhaps, as thinking is not my forté) that I'd do the same thing again. Kill me but leave those two kids alone. I really meant it, but then I didn't have a gun in my face or someone before me big enough to bludgeon me to death with his fists.

The man did get his release and showed up at church. Maybe it was God's spirit that I experienced no alarm or fear, even when he asked to meet me, just the two of us in a remote part of the building. His countenance had changed. There was openness, peace, and even joy that added up to more than release from prison. No eeriness. He had gotten freedom from an internal prison that put him in a real one.

He wanted to thank me for what I had done. He said he had gotten the help he needed. Honestly, I didn't feel it was necessary or feel any relief.

I couldn't help but ask, "Did you think about killing me when you were in prison?" He smiled and said nonchalantly, "I thought about it." No, my blood didn't run cold nor did I feel any relief. If anything, for some strange reason, I felt close to this person. We both laughed at something very serious.

The next time I heard the man speak was to a group of about twenty other men who knew he had gone to prison. He thanked me again and told the men I had saved his life.

His words moved me deeply, and I count what he said as a highlight in both lay ministry and my entire life.

I fail in so many areas, so many times. Included in those failures are situations where I was a coward. I'm ashamed of those times, and I doubt I'd ever muster enough bravery to even write about them.

I'd like to think a scripture imprinted on my soul caused me to do what was in front of me: "perfect love casts out fear" (1 John 4:18 NKJV). I never met the two kids this man victimized. But then I've never met Jesus in the flesh either. I don't have to meet either him or those two kids. I am

Cowardice, Courage, and Stupidity

the father of two daughters and now two granddaughters, and I would want someone to do the same for my girls.

I heard a question recently from a great Bible teacher that asked the question: What is your glory? I don't have a "glory," or at least I can't figure out what it is if there is one. Maybe protecting those two girls was my glory. I don't know. All I know is, I try to know the Lord in all my ways, and he takes care of directing my paths or at least the ones I allow him to. I'm glad he put me across the paths of a perpetrator and his victims.

And yes, I'm glad I'm still alive.

"Was Jesus frowning or smiling at you?"

Many years ago, I had to answer probably the most provocative and even startling question ever put to me. It came from a ministry workbook and caused me to lose, for a time, a lay ministry position helping addicts. The question was this: When you picture Jesus, is he frowning or smiling at you? One definition of a split-second is the time it took me to write down, "He's too far away for me to tell." That answer *should* disqualify you from ministry.

The workbook question came as an adult more than four decades from when, as a boy of five or six years old, I asked Jesus into my heart. A babushka-wearing immigrant from the Russian steppe, Catherine Semenko, my Sunday School teacher, led me to the Lord. Cathy's radiant, round face spoke of sheer joy and peace in being a child of God. What God had given her was irrepressible, expressed most vividly in how she'd clap her hands. She'd spread her hands wide apart and clasp more than clap them together, using not just her arms but her shoulders. She put her everything into it and not just her heart.

The first time I shared about Catherine, memories of this precious saint brought me to tears, and I've cried many times in the retelling. I left Catherine's Sunday School class feeling physically different and out into a world around me with colors more intense and a kind of glow over the mountains that surrounded me in West Virginia. I was truly a child of light after that experience.

That was, however, only over a short period of time. I had to look into the face daily of a dad whose deep-set, ice-blue eyes were cold with anger and restlessness. I never knew what he was thinking when he would look

"Was Jesus frowning or smiling at you?"

at me. I just know it wasn't approval or affection, and I felt, if not fear of him, a distance I couldn't close. I felt like I wasn't what he wanted or who he wanted to be with, and, like most children, I blamed myself. Something was wrong with me.

My own anger began to fester, and, as a child of God, I questioned why this same God, who would bring me into his light, would also give me this brooding, distant man and a home of darkness and tension. I didn't shift blame from myself, but I shared it with God. God, how could you give me this dad?

The separation and distance from God began with that question and continued for decades as I drifted away from him in adolescence and then adulthood.

My dad, and many other dads, told their sons in one way or another, intentionally or unintentionally, consciously or unconsciously, that we didn't measure up or we weren't good enough. The father of one close friend of mine actually told his son, "You'll never amount to anything." My friend became a basketball coach and has a high school state championship to his credit in basketball-mad Kentucky. My dad never told me I'd never amount to anything, but he may as well have. That's the unspoken message I seemed to get from him.

Men suffering from what author John Eldridge, in his great book, *Wild at Heart*, calls "dad wounds" retreat behind some persona of what a man is supposed to be, usually a stiff-upper-lip, pseudo-tough-guy façade that is a mask for deep insecurity. We become the "Marlboro man" from the old cigarette advertising, a lone cowboy out on the range. Ironically, this cowboy is also killing himself with cigarettes as he wanders the range alone on horseback.

Many, if not most of us men, go about our own range of isolation, killing ourselves with self-perceived weakness and fear. We are virtually mute, holding on to, or having it hold on to us, a deep-rooted belief that we'll "never amount to anything."

When I did begin a return to Jesus, I didn't *see* him, as there was an idol blocking the view. (That's for another time or actually one or more essays.)

The frowning-or-smiling question put my relationship with him into a whole new and blindingly clear perspective. I was a great, great distance from God.

To close the distance with my dad, education and then career achievement were my twin paths. I got a degree from the best university in my chosen profession. I had a genuine measure of success as an advertising copywriter, flying to New York and other cities to work on national and international accounts. Success and a culture among creatives in advertising caused me to adopt the obnoxious hipness and swagger that characterizes most copywriters and art directors in the business. I embraced all that, but it wasn't enough. I turned to substances to temporarily deaden the pain that success couldn't heal.

My dad never expressed his pride in me as he watched what I was doing in a career. Oh, he bragged to others but never said the first word to me. He also told me only once in my life "I love you," but that came, I believe, out of obligation as he'd just told my sister that. It was a "you too" kind of thing.

Today, I'm sober from everything, and when I say everything, I mean *everything*—drugs, alcohol, sex, and anything else possibly addictive.

More importantly, I've forgiven a dad who I think suffered from a very serious wound of his own.

Forgiveness can't replace forgetting, however, and words and actions are things that, once spoken or done, are permanently irretrievable.

I read something many, many years ago and have never forgotten it because of its truth in my life: a man can never be truly at peace until his father is dead. Part of that is true. There may be *some* peace but not *full* peace.

Despite the maxim above, I miss my dad, remembering the good and even great things about him, most discovered and appreciated after I became an adult. I'm mindful, too, of the struggles he had. The Bible says "But he will not leave the guilty unpunished, bringing the consequences of the fathers' iniquity on the children to the third and fourth generation" (Num 14:18 CSB). That is truth. But God forgives sin and remembers it not. And I'm supposed to do the same thing.

My dad is from another generation, that of World War II and men who fought in a horrific war who learned to internalize things probably to keep from going insane.

It's been a long journey but today, I see Jesus. I see him throwing his head back and laughing with mouth wide open out of my delight with the wife he led me to. I also see him smile with satisfaction at my gratitude for something small to me that was large to him. (I recently prayed to be writing again for a magazine I had written for several years ago, and he

"Was Jesus frowning or smiling at you?"

answered that prayer.) I also see him—and this is what is most important—stricken on a cross, beaten beyond human recognition, seeing through eyes having to blink back blood and tears. Somewhere along the line, he gently led me into seeing him.

Away from that horrible cross, when I see him in my mind, he smiles at me. But more often than not, I think he laughs at me—how I express myself, the joy I take in the fellowship of the many spiritual brothers he has given me, how much I love these brothers of mine, all the things that show him I am a chip off the proverbial block . . . his "block" made in his likeness.

I recently watched a small group of Christian men share questions they would ask of non-believers to bring them into consideration of giving their hearts to Jesus. With most people, my question would be, "So when did you and God fall out?" Something usually causes separation—the death of a loved one, a tragedy, an injustice, a dad or mom wound, and much more. I fell out with God because of my dad.

The second question, though, is the big one: Who is Jesus to you? I think you start at the end rather than the beginning—the man on the cross, working back to what he did and said in his time on the earth. In truth, the end of his human life on earth is our beginning. From the moment he said, "It is finished" he obliterated the distance between us and God. I can see him clearly.

Seeing him, however, isn't as simple as believing the truth of what he did on a cross, or marveling at how an eight-inch thick, eighty-foot-tall curtain separating the Holy of Holies in the Jerusalem temple split from top to bottom at his death, signifying the end of separation from God. We can all know these things but it must become personal: coming to know Jesus through whatever means he leads us into.

I write in the next essay of God literally "smarting off" to me when I asked him something in prayer. I see him not smiling, but adopting a look of what I expressed as "feigned annoyance." I've never felt closer to God through this expression of familiarity and comfort with my company. Teasing is usually a sign of affection. To be teased by God? Wow. Jesus doesn't just love me, he *likes* me. He sees me, and he always has, from Aunt Cathy's Sunday School to an unhappy home alongside a creek in a West Virginia hollow to all he has brought me to in my life.

He always could see me even when I couldn't see him.

"Look it up yourself."

I think we often miss something when we hear we're "made in the image of God." Think about this: God maybe looks like us, but here's the shocker: he, at times, *acts* like us. He has human qualities, specifically, all the emotions we have. In fact, he *created* those emotions, and he exercises them just like we do.

A long time ago I paid the monthly mortgage of a family member when they were in financial straits at what I felt and believed was God's direction. No problem . . . for the first six months. After that, my flesh got the best of me and I decided to go to God in prayer asking, "How long is this going to go on?" I would even say I became maybe a little bold, addressing him perhaps irreverently as in "Hey God, look, this is getting old. So how long, huh?" His answer was clear as a bell: "It is easier for a camel to go through the eye of a needle than for a rich man to enter the kingdom of God" (Matt 19:24 NKJV). Whooaa-kay, thank you very much, God. Never mind my asking.

"So how long" was going to be until he directed me differently and he may as well have said "so long" to me given what happened next.

You'll have to trust me on this, but I remember thinking and praying, "Since we're talking, I got another question." I don't remember what it was except I asked him for the scripture that would answer it. Here's where you *really* have to trust me: His response was, "You've got a Concordance; look it up yourself." (A Concordance is an alphabetical index of words providing original Hebrew and Greek words and their translations for the Old Testament and New Testament, respectively.) He talked to me in the same way I

"Look it up yourself."

had addressed him, not in a tit-for-tat exchange, but speaking my language and knowing it would bless me hugely.

This absolutely cracked me up, and I treasure the "conversation" decades later. I could picture him, complete with feigned annoyance and irritation. If I heard from him like Moses, a mighty voice from heaven with the sound of thunder, I could not have been more blessed to hear him kind of smart-off to me. He knew what I would appreciate.

For this reason, I love a story from the Old Testament in Exodus chapter thirty-two. Moses is on the mountaintop and God needs to alert him that the Hebrews have built a golden calf while he's been away. The words God uses are straight out of the classic mother/father script when a child or children are disobedient. "Go down at once! For *your* people who *you* brought up from the land of Egypt have acted corruptly" (Exod 32:7 CSB). (italics added) God sounds just like any other parent. It's *your* son or *your* daughter when they misbehave.

It gets better from there: God is done, I mean *d-o-n-e* with the disobedience and complaining of these people for whom he's parted the Red Sea, led with visible pillars of fire and cloud, and fed with manna.

> *"The Lord also said to Moses: I have seen this people, and they are indeed a stiff-necked people.*
>
> *"Now leave me alone, so that my anger can burn against them and I can destroy them. Then I will make you into a great nation."* (Exod 32:9-10 CSB)

God is completely exasperated, saying to Moses basically, "Look, I've had it. I'm wiping them out, and you and I will start over."

The expression "cooler heads prevailed" is appropriate for what's next, but the surprise is who had the cooler head. Long before Isaiah wrote "come now and let us reason together" (Isa 1:17 NKJV) Moses makes a great case before God:

> *"Why should the Egyptians say, 'He brought them out with an intent to kill them in the mountains and eliminate them from the face of the earth? Remember your servants Abraham, Isaac, and Israel— you swore to them by yourself and declared, 'I will make your offspring as numerous as the stars of the sky and will give your offspring all this land that I have promised, and they will inherit it forever.'"* (Exod 32:12-13 CSB)

Moses reminds him, to use common language, "Look, your reputation is going to be shot. Think about it: You lead these people by a miracle out of Egypt and, because they act like idiots out here, you kill them all. Not a good look, if you don't mind my saying so."

Again, we know that we are, as the scriptures say, made in the image of God. But he's made, apparently, more like us than we realize, reflecting himself to us in "humanness." Was God testing Moses? Considering he could have started over with Moses, I'm not so sure. None of us will know until we get to heaven.

All I do know is, it is just plain fun to see him looking just like us. That draws me closer to him, makes him more approachable, and maybe, at some time in the future, sets me up for another look-it-up-yourself exchange.

I hope so.

God Works in Mysterious Ways

The old saying "God works in mysterious ways, His wonders to behold" is just that, a saying, and not in the Bible, which might surprise a lot of us. (It comes from a hymn.) But maybe it ought to be in the Bible.

Case in point: Of all things, God uses a serpent to communicate with Moses in the desert. And this isn't a talking serpent like the one in the Garden of Eden, but the normal biting kind.

Maybe stunned by a voice coming from a burning bush, Moses asks for a sign that it really is God in Exodus chapter four. God tells him to throw down his rod, which transforms into a serpent. Maybe most of us would have taken the hint that a voice coming from a bush on fire but not consumed is God. All of us, though, would do as Moses did: He ran from the snake before getting his wits about him and returning to it. Slowly and carefully, I would guess.

God tells him to pick it up and it transforms back into his rod. (Whew!)

Lots of symbolism here: The rod was Moses' shepherd's crook, the tool of his profession. I assign a lot of meaning to him throwing down his crook, his tool used for making a living. What does God ask of us? Our all—heart, soul, mind, body . . . our *life*. Shepherding, at the time, was Moses' life.

God wasn't finished using that same rod, either. Moses used it when God parted the Red Sea, pointing it at the waters. God also brought forth water from a rock when he told Moses to strike it with his rod.

Moses deserves a lot of credit here. First, I wouldn't have stopped running after my rod turned into a snake. (A snake? Are you kidding? This *has* to be the devil!) Second, he's confident enough that he is hearing from God to pick up the snake. That's courage I don't have.

Who can know the mind of God, or his mysterious ways, or what he has in mind using a serpent, but I'll advance a theory: In Moses' case, I think God wanted to test his obedience in situations completely out of his control. Think about it: Who's in control when encountering a snake? You can control your flight and the speed with which you flee, but that's about it. God tells him not only to pick it up but also to pick it up by its tail—the last thing you want to do. Yep, it's a snake, but it's in the control of God Almighty.

In a way, it was a test of the leadership God wanted from Moses. Think about leading two million people through a desert: He leaves them to go up on a mountaintop to hear from God and they build a golden calf. Never mind they had walked through a Red Sea that miraculously parted and ate manna daily that fell from heaven for their sustenance. An out-of-control lot to be sure. Moses had to trust God to lead these people, unable to control the grumbling and complaining and idol-building. He had to depend on God who, by the way, got so fed up with his people he wanted to destroy them and start over again just with Moses in Exodus chapter thirty-two (an idea Moses talked him out of).

God wants control, but he has to trust us to give over our control to him. When we as humans try to wrest control from God for our decisions, that is when we get into trouble. Moses trusted God and obviously, God made a good decision in choosing him to lead his people.

God also wants our attention and focus on all things. I have to think Moses, even though he was hearing the voice of God, never took his eyes off the serpent. A snake, after all, is still a snake, the voice of God notwithstanding.

The serpent encounter is critical in the life of Moses and God's people. Had Moses decided to keep running from his rod-turned-serpent he would have never fulfilled his destiny. Yet he trusted God, turning over a scary situation to a God whose thoughts and actions are beyond our understanding and comprehension. Mysterious, from the hymn, is the right word.

When we take on God's will, purpose, and role for our life, he requires us to be all-trusting, to know that whatever he tells us to do, if it is his will, it will be all right, and he will see us through it. Personally, I can't imagine being obedient to pick up a snake alive or dead, but then I'm not called to lead two million people through a desert.

One final thought: Wasn't there something else besides a serpent God could have used to show God's power to Moses? It's a good question to ask,

I think. Here's my answer: I don't think so. Nothing could command the respect and attention of a serpent, and finally, the trust in God needed to pick it up.

Mystery solved.

Cigars and Ink Pens

I've always credited the book *Search for Significance* and a workshop at my church based on it as the first step toward some huge, much-needed changes in my life. My sole memory of the workshop, however, is of a well-meaning believer handing me an ink pen to witness to me. I was and am a believer, but he didn't ask if I was, launching instead into a canned spiel I knew he had used with people before. (I must have been giving off some kind of "sinner vibe.")

I thought about this as I was getting ready to give a cigar to a non-believing co-worker. Similar shape to an ink pen, worlds apart in the message. I like this co-worker. I had already given him a cigar before, which he appreciated. I wanted to show him God's kindness. Maybe, just maybe, this would somehow open a door for him to know I am a believer, for him to be curious, and for him to find God. Who knows?

What I do know is that the guy with the ink pen, again, didn't know me. And handing me a pen didn't translate into a sincere concern for my heart and eternal destiny. To me, it was a rote message and nothing more. I won't go so far as to say he was a Christian "gunslinger," aiming to get another notch on his belt, but I have that suspicion. I've seen them.

I felt like an experiment in an exercise to see if something—the spiel—would work or work again. I felt anything but *significant*.

I don't know; the ink pen shtick might be just the thing for an unbeliever. I know what *isn't*, though: an encounter that passes even the merest shadow of judgment on a non-believer. "You need Jesus," as true as I may believe it is for all of us, can carry messages: You're not who or what you're supposed to be. You're lacking. You're missing something. And worst of all:

because *I* have Jesus, you're not as good as me, or you should be like me. All the preceding carries both blatant and inherent judgment. Who likes to be judged, especially by a perfect stranger?

Evangelism, quite frankly, escapes me. I was once part of a church that had a booth at the state fair. Members had to take one-hour time slots handing out tracts to those passing by. My wife and I took slots, her going right before me. I'll never forget what she asked me, returning to the booth after my shift: "You hated it, didn't you?" Yep. I was practically throwing tracts at people rather than passing them out at the end of the hour, and I don't think I talked to a single person. I've always said, let somebody else catch the fish; I'll do the "cleaning"—teaching and encouraging. Seriously. Somebody's got to do it, first of all, and second, fish cleaning is what some people, like myself, actually prefer.

All believers should evangelize, but a lot of us, if not most of us, only think of direct, "here's-an-ink-pen" kind of stuff. Saint Francis gets credit for saying "preach the Gospel always, and, when necessary, use words." Wow. Now that opens a whole new world with a far bigger scope for evangelism.

The story of Zacchaeus in the sycamore tree became a children's story, I think, because of that little song taught to kids in Sunday School. I won't repeat any of the lyrics here, and you probably just got an earworm reading this. I know I did writing about it just now.

There's more to explore here than meets the eye and a real example of evangelism. Firstly, Zacchaeus, a "wee little man" (I broke my promise) was also, most assuredly, the most despised man in his community. He was a tax collector for the Romans, making him a traitor to his people and a collaborator with an occupying enemy in the land. On top of being a sell-out, he was a thief. Tax collectors gouged the people as much as possible over and above required taxes to profit from the position.

One question would be, why would Zacchaeus want to see this Jesus guy who preached charity to the poor? Not only that, but he went to the trouble and difficulty of getting up in a tree to get a good look at him. He was short, yes, but was that the reason? He wasn't welcome in any public setting so there was a risk in being conspicuous, drawing attention to himself perched above the crowd. Or maybe he was trying to be inconspicuous.

The second question is, did Jesus know him before then? Had he paid taxes of his own to Zacchaeus? Did he know Zacchaeus by reputation? Or, as the Son of God, did he know him because, well, he created him?

But Jesus addresses him by name and here's where the King James or any other version needs some adjectives or details, in my opinion. What was the tone when he spoke, "'Zacchaeus, make haste and come down, for today I must stay at your house'" (Luke 19:5 NKJV)? I think that probably loses everything in translation. I imagine a friendly, maybe even gregarious savior looking up in the tree, acting as if he wasn't expecting to see someone up there, and saying something along these lines: "Hey, Zacchaeus, dinner at your house later. Me and you." (Ok, maybe not those words, but not the King James either.)

I have a friend and a former adult porn star who, standing outside a strip bar drinking vodka, heard God speak to him by name. That took away any doubt for David that he was hearing from God. It touched his life and transformed it in an instant. God knew this man and he let him know it.

Zacchaeus became an honest man and later returned the overpayment of tax money to people.

There are a lot of parallels between my friend outside the strip bar and Zacchaeus besides God knowing them by name. My friend, like Zacchaeus, was as far out of the mainstream of society as you can get. And hearing God's voice was as big a surprise to him as it may have been to Zacchaeus.

The invitation from Jesus was "Hey Zacchaeus, I accept you as you are, and I want a relationship with you." No threat. No judgment. No, "Zacchaeus, you're a tax collector and you need to repent. You need me." Only a desire to meet and to love Zacchaeus. He accepts Zacchaeus where he is and looks past occupation, reputation, and all the rest.

Jesus said, "Let your light so shine before men" (Matt 5:16 NKJV). The Gospel of John refers to Jesus as "light." Light doesn't expose darkness but changes it into light. Our task in evangelizing is not to expose the darkness in others, but to show light.

Or, in my case, to give them a light to their cigar.

Jesus is Lord Over Shreveport

If you get a speeding ticket in my home state of Kentucky you can pay the full amount of a fine or pay a substantially lesser amount and go to a four-hour "traffic school." Anyone who has gone will tell you, sometimes it's better to just pay the fine. It is almost always very boring and not worth the savings.

Of the several times I've gone (!), I've been fortunate to have had some actually entertaining instructors. I guess they're trying to beat their own boredom with the school, and one guy, I seriously think, may have been working on a career as a comedian.

As much as attendees try to tune it out and just get through a long evening or Saturday morning, there are some inevitable takeaways. Mine, on one of my school trips, was an instructor saying we respond in one of three ways to a mistake we see another driver make: parent, child, or adult.

I couldn't help but think of this with something that happened one day driving in an unfamiliar city. This was in the days before cell phones, GPS navigation, and that annoying but useful voice telling you every turn to make. Back in the day, you flew into a city, got a map from the rental car folks, and figured it out, following highlighter markings. I was always proud of my ability to navigate practically anywhere (except for Washington, D.C., which threw me for literal loops). Mistakes, however, were inevitable, and one day, entering a freeway, I made one that I was sure was going to bring on a honking horn, shaking fist, or worse from a driver whose car I almost hit.

As the driver went by me, however, with none of these responses I expected—not even a disgusted shaking of the head—something spoke up on the inside of me, "This person must be a believer." It was no surprise to me and was, in fact, a blessing to see a bumper sticker on the car that read "Jesus is Lord over Shreveport."

This driver demonstrated his walk with the Lord in a very striking way, at least to me. It might have something to do with my having zero grace for the mistakes of others on the highway. (More on this below.)

I can't help but think how a non-believer would respond to that kind of grace, seeing the bumper sticker and how someone might also react if there had been a honking horn, a shaking fist, or a fist with one finger raised.

The near-accident is something I'll never forget for good reasons and bad. First the bad: To say I have little grace for other drivers making mistakes on the road is an epic understatement. I will freely admit I've interrupted prayer, as I drive, with vile epithets for offending drivers not fit for any place save a biker bar. Let's just say I'm proof that, according to James 3:10 (NKJV), "Out of the same mouth proceed blessing and cursing." I also have a bad answer to the question in the next verse, James 3:11 (NKJV) "Does a spring send forth fresh water and bitter from the same opening?". Apparently, it can, at least from my own well. I would even say I don't respond as a parent, child, or adult but one of those names I've called other drivers.

The good reason I won't forget the near-accident and bumper sticker is that it is a reminder that Jesus should not just be "Lord over Shreveport" over yours truly on the highways there but everywhere. If Jesus is my Lord, there should be a fourth response we can choose in dealing with strangers besides acting like a parent, child, adult, or any obscenity: grace-filled believer.

Angels Unawares

I've "attended angels unawares" referred to in the Book of Hebrews 13:2 (KJV) twice, I'm pretty sure, and definitely once.

The "once" was when I was a kid. We lived next to a very large railroad yard maybe within fifty yards of my house with round-the-clock noise from train diesel engines loud enough for us not to be able to sleep in relative silence when we would travel. My mom and dad never knew that I would hitch rides on slow-moving coal trains to get from one end of Wilcoe Yard, my neighborhood, to the other end where my friend Larry lived.

This was the 1950's when moms stayed home, and it was unusual for her not to be in the house, particularly around dinner time, and very unusual for me to be alone. I don't know where I was going or what I was going to do but it involved a railroad lantern, which we kept in the kitchen. As I bent over to pick it up, a strong voice came from my parent's bedroom— "No." I looked into the open door of the bedroom knowing it and the rest of the house was empty. I left the lantern where it sat. Why I believe it was an angel was the voice didn't startle me, even though it was firm and delivered with above-normal volume. I will always believe the voice saved me from death either by a train or something else.

It's not as clear-cut with the other two occasions of angelic visitation. One was a "lowlight" in my relationship with my dad.

The opening day of trout fishing in West Virginia is right up there with Christmas Day for adults and kids. Anglers line the banks of streams watching the sweep hand on watches till its 6:00 a.m. to drop hooks into the water. It is, or was, a very big deal, rivaling the opening day of deer season in the mountains.

In my innocence, I was excited about the day, which became the first and last day I ever went trout fishing with my dad. It began with an unsettling ride to Panther Creek in southern West Virginia with a couple of his co-workers. I was maybe six years old and raised in the Pentecostal Holiness religion. I distinctly remember the conversation covering a sex act with a euphemism I cannot share here. At my age, I didn't know there was such a sex act, but I knew somehow that what they were talking about was bad. Also, my dad became quiet. Looking back, I think he got into that kind of conversation at work.

The magic moment arrived for fishing . . . and my hook and line tangled in a tree above me. Before you ask if I want cheese with my whine, dear reader, know that what followed was part of a pattern that has taken a lot of therapy and more of God's healing to overcome.

I was in a panic to get the line out of the tree probably as much to keep my dad from getting mad as anything. He did something worse than getting mad: he ignored me to not miss one second of his fishing.

My memory should focus on what happened next, and I thank God I've grown in grace enough to make it the highlight of the memory and to see God in it: A man whose countenance was unforgettable came to my rescue.

I believe I saw this same man (angel?) decades later.

The father of my ex-wife struggled financially and drove an old "beater." It broke down one night on an entrance ramp to a freeway. There were no homes nearby and I'm not sure you could even see the car, my wife, my father-in-law, and me from businesses close to the ramp. A man appeared out of nowhere. He popped the hood, fixed what was wrong with no tools, and just kind of disappeared. Age may be playing tricks on me here, but I think it was the same angel who helped me that day trout fishing. This, more than the fishing-line rescue, is most likely to have been an angel. There was nowhere for this man to have come from, and he disappeared into nowhere just as quickly.

Whether you believe all three events involved an angel or just two or just one, God's Word says unequivocally "some have entertained angels unawares."

It's difficult what to make of angelic visitations because of the word "unawares." The voice saying "No" doesn't qualify, it would seem, under the

Angels Unawares

scripture as I was definitely aware that it came from someone invisible in my house. At the same time, the Bible says we have guardian angels.

The thing that sticks with me is how unforgettable the experiences were. I believe there are lessons from these incidences that are there for teaching. The lesson from the voice is simple and obvious: God protects us and will keep us from harm until his appointed time to join him in heaven. The incident with the car and the mysterious stranger who appeared is strangely moving, and that's all I can say about that. Why I can't forget it is because I wasn't *meant* to forget it.

The tangled fishing line has a message that has taken me years to finally get to. I have grace and forgiveness for a dad who did his best under the circumstances. He was a deeply wounded man rejected far more openly and hurtfully, perhaps, than I was by him. He could only model what was before him when he was a kid. But he also did things like expose me to the world—New York City primarily, a 'fer piece' from the West Virginia coalfields—that set a course for my life, a good course. I love to tell people of my dad's insistence with school authorities over strenuous objections that they excuse, in one case, an absence of more than a week of school so I could be with him in New York City on one of his business trips. Now that's a good if not great father.

I thank God for what fathering I did get. Many men had it worse. But what I really thank God for is the grace he gave me to forgive my dad ... and untangling a fishing line, fixing a car, and keeping me from an accident or death.

"Be still . . ."

My "prayer closet" is an interstate highway I travel weekdays to my job and back. I'll confess something shocking to a lot of believers, understood by others, and admitted to, probably, by very few: I don't like to pray. I'd much rather listen to sports-talk radio. Still, as I hit the entrance ramp each weekday, I start with "Good morning, daddy God." And, on two occasions, I have followed that up mindlessly with, "How are you?" — the most ridiculous question ever uttered to anyone anywhere. I continue for a whole nine minutes till I pull onto the exit ramp. For me, that's a major accomplishment to pray that long at one time.

I equate prayer, for me, to small children brushing their teeth: it's generally disliked early on by kids, but becomes something, over time, we can't do without as we grow up. Apparently, I am still a "baby believer" after forty years, because I never have gotten to where prayer isn't a task. At the same time, I know it is something I can't do without.

My prayer is pretty much the same daily: to be a good husband to my wife; for my children and their spouses; stepchildren and grandchildren; for the company that employs me; for men friends of mine and their wives. That's about it, and all of the above are subject to sporadic deletion.

One day it occurred to me God knows the list from my repetition not to mention he is all-knowing. I sometimes am silent on the short ride on the interstate. Do I hear from God? Not yet, or that I can tell. But I like to think I open my spirit to him in that quiet time.

I can say that somehow, someway, the silence has seemed to bring me a revelation of the Holy Spirit as a person. I'm not talking about a spiritual entity but a person like you'd see on the street—a male with sandy hair,

"Be still . . ."

and, well, a *comforting* countenance. ("But the Comforter, which is the Holy Ghost . . . " [John 14:26 NKJV]). He is identical, in my mind, to the man who I believe was an angel that appeared to me twice—once as a boy and a second time as an adult.

He's comforting enough that, like an old friend, I can ride in a car with him without conversation.

On occasion, I will talk to him and ask him to help me with something, but a lot of the time I remain silent.

Interaction with God—Father, Son, and Holy Spirit—seems to emphasize, for most of us, the second half of the word: inter*action*. We work hard to hear from God—what it is he wants us to do, what is going on, what he's doing to "direct our paths," to borrow from the familiar verse in Proverbs. And the sooner the better. Never mind that we are to "Be still, and know that I am God" (Ps 46:10 NKJV). I'm not the brightest bulb in the row and, as you've probably already surmised I'm sure, I'm not the most disciplined believer, but I understand that being still means, at times, being silent. And if being still gets us direction or answers, then let's get on with it. Being still also precludes clenched teeth and intense concentration to tune in to God, as if that's going to help.

What helped me and could help others like me is to get to the real meaning of "still," as used by David in Psalm 46:10. The Hebrew root word, *raphah*, means simply "to slacken." Other, surprising meanings from the Concordance of Hebrew and Greek words in the Bible are "to fail," "be faint," "be feeble," "forsake," "be slack," "be slothful" (?!), and finally, to "be weak."

It should be apparent why it is so difficult for any of us to be still, actually.

It goes against our very nature to fail; to be faint, feeble, or slothful; or, God forbid, be weak. We are, after all, children of the King, overcomers and "more than conquerors through him who loves us" (Romans 8:37 KJV). Yet his word also tells us that, "for my strength is made perfect in weakness" (2 Cor 12:9 NKJV).

Interestingly, this "Be still" scripture and my search into its meaning began with a friend attempting to point me toward my powerlessness—a great word for weakness—in a certain situation. It involved, in just a few words, inner healing that points to a second, perhaps more familiar, meaning of the word *raphah*. This is one of the names given God or Jehovah by the Hebrews, and it means "healer." Just as we would sit "still" while any medical doctor examines us to heal our physical wounds, so God wants us to be still while he heals the situations, circumstances, and wounds that afflict us in life.

I believe that David knew exactly what he was writing when he chose this particular meaning of the word "still" among multiple meanings. Yes, there are times when God will have us do certain things and speak to us what those things are in even an audible, unmistakable voice. More are the times, though, when we grind teeth in concentration to be still, doing our absolute best to hear from God.

The Serenity Prayer that is a cornerstone for the philosophy/quasi-theology of Alcoholics Anonymous asks of God that he grants the serenity *to accept the things I cannot change, the courage to change the things I can, and the wisdom to know the difference.* May we know and have the serenity to know the times when we can accept our weakness and powerlessness. And know the times when we are to be still.

Gambling

(or let your "Yes" be "Yes", and your "No" be "No")

I heard someone once say that the problem with trying to follow God in day-to-day life is that everybody has his or her own set of rules for how they should behave. This breeds what I call legalism and hypocrisy to the hilt. We'll judge others for not following our set of rules while we allow things in our life others may judge as sin.

We all, to one degree or another, are legalistic. That is, there are things we probably don't do, not so much because our conscience or an inner witness forbids it, but because it gives us a sense of righteousness, a word missing four letters and a hyphen: *self*-righteousness.

It's all about us, kind of like the story of the Pharisee in Luke 18 who thanks God he isn't like other men—extortionists, unjust adulterers, etc. In short, he's saying he's glad he's better than everyone else. He goes so far as to compare himself to a tax collector he sees near him, talking about how he fasts twice a week and tithes. The tax collector on the other hand beats his breast, saying "God, be merciful to me a sinner" (Luke 18:13 NKJV). Jesus said the tax collector went to his home justified while the Pharisee didn't.

Whether it's self-righteousness or God, I don't gamble at golf. Curse, yes. I admit it. And a lot, too, not just on the golf course. Gamble, no. (Remember what I said about we all have our own set of rules.) Yep, it's true. I will add that I inadvertently touched on a sensitive subject when I jokingly suggested to my pastor one day that I promised not to curse if he promised not to gamble. I didn't know it was a sensitive subject with many church members whose personal rules forbade gambling on golf and knew their pastor did so. You'll never guess who held up their end of the bargain. The pastor, as fine as they come, wouldn't have thought of a round of golf without a dollar on the winner of the front nine, back nine, and overall. And I can think of few Christians I've golfed with who haven't wanted to put a dollar "just for fun" on the results. As best as I can recall, I didn't curse, which means I probably played fairly well.

I don't gamble for a simple reason: if I win, I'm taking something that doesn't belong to me but someone else. Never mind that they agreed to risk it, or gamble with their money. I'm still taking something that is theirs. (Of course, I'll put down a bet at the racetrack, not against the track, but everybody around me, breaking, obviously, my own rule.)

Legalism also has another funny quirk to it besides everyone having their own set of dos and don'ts: Nobody can stick to their own rules. I didn't one Saturday and learned, if not a valuable lesson monetarily speaking, at least a lesson taught from the Bible.

Going to the course alone one day without a pre-arranged foursome I hooked up with a pleasant enough man and his teenage son. It was a beautiful day, I was playing better than usual, and, as it seems to always be, golf is a great common denominator between strangers that produces an instant, if temporary bond. In short, the golf was good and so was the company . . . through the first nine holes.

As we prepared to tee off on the back nine the man suggested we put a dollar on the results. Without hesitation, I replied, "I don't gamble." He was incredulous and voiced his disbelief loudly. As much to escape what became a slightly uncomfortable situation, and giving in to the argument "it's only a dollar," I gave in.

The mood of the whole round changed at that point. Without a word spoken, serious competition entered the atmosphere. The man's son, perhaps taking a cue from his dad, rudely asked me if I was "choking" after a series of bad shots on my part. In short, a very pleasant day in the company of strangers (and golf is the one thing that can bring strangers together better than anything) ended in a struggle for one-upmanship and conquest of one competitor over another. All over four quarters, ten dimes, twenty nickels, one-hundred pennies.

It ruined everything.

What I did was violate my own rules along with God's instruction: "'But let your 'Yes' mean 'Yes,' and your 'No' mean 'No'" (Matt 5:37 NKJV). At some point in the fellow golfer's borderline harangue to goad me into a

Gambling

bet, he even made a crude, off-color speculation about my religion. At that point, I should have said, "You know, I am a follower of Jesus Christ, and I don't gamble at golf." I imagine that would have ended it. I compromised with the world and worse, I compromised my principles.

You can probably guess who lost the bet.

The Color of All

In my phone photos, I have a picture of a swarthy brown man with short dark hair, deep brown eyes, and a beard not closely cropped, but not long either. The photo came from a Google search for an image of a "typical Galilean man of Jesus' time." Narrative accompanying the picture detailed how men of that time kept their hair short.

I think Jesus looked nothing like the painted images we have of him. No blue eyes. No flowing, light-brown hair. He was a Semite of Israel. Think of an Arab-looking man and there you have him.

Hollywood misses it more than artists from the past. Case in point: the movie *Ben Hur*, produced way back in 1959 but cherished through the years by many Christian believers. (As late as the 1980s I went to a "*Ben Hur* Movie Night" at the home of someone in my church.) Without question, it is the most egregious, off-the-mark representation of Jesus in twenty-one centuries. The scene where Jesus appears in this altogether good if not great movie is borderline comical: You see a dusty, dirty village with drably dressed people going here and there, and then there's this tall, striking man in a brilliant white robe and long, conditioned and coiffed hair. It's ridiculous. The film's director does the audience a favor, however, of not showing the face of the actor playing Jesus, sparing us, probably, a Fabio lookalike.

That's Hollywood, and they're seldom going to get it right, it seems, when it comes to things Christian. But then their visual reference and cultural conditioning for Jesus are centuries-old paintings depicting, well, a blue-eyed Gentile.

How did he become a "Gentile Jesus"? Wow, that's a question to ponder.

The Color of All

I have a theory that the "Gentilization" of Jesus was marketing by painting masters. They had to satisfy religious and political leaders decidedly anti-Semitic and anti-Judaism. (Thank you, Constantine, Justin Martyr, and other well-known anti-Semites.)

Anti-Semitism at the top of the religious and political hierarchy more than likely influenced their flocks and constituencies. It's not hard to imagine that folks might have been more apt to accept a Jesus who looked like them, pure and simple. And behind that, I think, is racism, *impure* and simple. I deeply believe racism is part of our sin nature. We are born not just with a preference for those whom we look like, but fear of someone different. And that can lead to hate.

A study done at an Ivy League school of babies some years ago revealed something interesting and innate: When Caucasian babies had to choose between a white baby doll or an African-American one offered to them, they chose the white and vice-versa. We gravitate—*segregate*, if you will—toward the familiar.

Jesus was God but also a Semite man.

For reasons so deep in my heart they're unexplainable, my eyes will sometimes fill up with tears when I think that, if you came upon a group of thirteen men, walking a road through Israel in the time of Jesus, you would have to ask, Which one is Jesus? Isaiah wrote, "He has no form or comeliness; And when we see Him, There is no beauty that we should desire Him" (Isa 53:2 NKJV).

Is it important we get real about what Jesus looked like? In this day and age, I think so. Today, politicians who can gain from divisions, pit the races against one another.

The joke is on us in a way. Where Jesus is concerned, he was neither black nor white. Brown has somehow escaped the vernacular of race discussion. He was not black or white.

He was *all*.

On the Mountain before me

"Over every mountain, there is a path, although it may not be seen from the valley."

THEODORE ROETHKE

Joseph's Sentence and My Own Time as a Slave

Beginning sometime in 2000 I entered a career desert of mammoth proportions, at least in length. It lasted till November of 2012. In that time, I went through agonizing and countless bouts of depression, saw God conquer an idol in my life, had the Government seize a bank account, had time to be a father to a son, borrowed money one year from a friend so my kids could have Christmas, sold blood plasma for my family to eat, and wondered the whole time when or if it was all going to end. In case you missed it, two good things happened in there. Those things were huge but, in my human state, the bad completely overshadowed them. I was a slave to poverty.

I remember once finding out I was the loser as a finalist for a job I desperately needed and lying on the cold concrete floor of my basement. It was the lowest place physically I could find. Spiritually and physically, I wanted to be *under* that hard floor. I wanted my body to be as cold in death as that concrete. My basic prayer to God, and I'm not making this up, was "Can I catch a break?!" That was all I could bring myself to pray for most of those twelve years. Seriously.

I know there are trials and seasons, times when the "heavens are brass," as I've heard it said. Small wonder that as a new believer, I strangely liked the Book of Job for reasons I didn't understand. I never knew I'd go through a trial similar, though infinitesimally smaller, than Job's.

I'll never forget a friend loaning me a pretty good book entitled *Job's Wife*. Gushing about it, she asked me with excitement after I had read it,

"Don't you feel like you *know* Job's wife?" My response drew a laugh but was honest: "Hell, I know *Job*."

Life looking up at the bottom (and not *at* the bottom itself, mind you) was not the norm or part of some pattern. I attended the best journalism school in the country at the University of Missouri, embarked on a career as an advertising copywriter and creative director that earned me both awards and good money, and managed marketing for the U.S. branch of a French conglomerate, which took me to Paris a couple of times for a week each trip.

The bottom began to fall out with a move from the French company to the vice-presidency of an advertising agency scant months away from bankruptcy. I didn't board the Titanic but one of the *lifeboats*. That place was taking on water well before I got there.

I rebounded briefly with a couple of successful years with my own business and then *phhtt* . . . nil, nada, nothing. Well, not exactly if you count day labor with homeless people and drug addicts for $5 an hour and working a third shift at a printing plant for $8 an hour. A short-lived return to good money, copywriting in an ad agency at the end of the decade, preceded the desert.

It's been nine years since leaving the desert and even then, the "send-off" from desert to deliverance was my wife of twenty-nine years and mother of our three children divorcing me. Why not keep the streak going right up to the very end, right?

We're all to take heart from something or someone in the Bible. For me, it's Joseph, son of Jacob. My desert was twelve years. Joseph's imprisonment for a crime he didn't commit—the attempted rape of his boss's wife—was around that long, either eleven or twelve years.

He was a good man with great character if not intellect. (How smart is it to run naked from a woman's house screaming, "I didn't do anything!"?) But he did everything else right, pretty much. Sharing the dreams of his brothers bowing down to him may have not been the smartest move, but the dreams were true, as it turned out, and it wasn't his fault his father favored him above his brothers. Think too, that Joseph, at the prime age for virility of eighteen, resisted the advances of a beautiful woman. I resisted *celibacy* before that age and afterward like that was something to be ashamed of.

Joseph's Sentence and My Own Time as a Slave

Who does Joseph have to blame for his false imprisonment and sale into slavery by his brothers? You'd have to say God, as there was a plan evident in all this to bring Joseph to a good end.

Who do I have to blame? Let's just say the prelude to my poverty—my own business in the '90's—was a matter of basically not playing well with others combined with delusions of grandeur.

God used the desert time, however, to conquer an idol in my life, but that's for another time and another essay (and it's already in my first book).

I know God also used it to parent my son, or at least I filled a lot of my time doing so. I treasure the time I spent with him, particularly helping him develop into a baseball player good enough to get a college scholarship. But there were bad times too, like the time when he watched me get angry hitting golf balls badly, and said, "Daddy, it's ok that you lost your job." Kids don't miss a thing and don't ever think they do. They're also not supposed to take care of their parents, and I hate that he did his best to do just that.

No, I don't write this from a foreign palace where I am Prime Minister. Instead, it *is* from a place I thought I'd never be. I have a good job with a great salary. I'm remarried to a beautiful and wonderful woman who loves God. I have a little money in the bank. I'm going to have a retirement I never thought I would have. And most important, I'm closer to God than I've ever been.

Reduced to selling blood plasma is the lowest point of all I went through, I guess, and the crooks of my arms bear these deep scars left by large, big-diameter needles. Those holes will never go away in this life anyway.

Jesus had scars on his hands and feet too. I had never thought about it until now, but he just as easily could have resurrected without those scars. He surely didn't need a reminder of what he'd been through but the disciples, perhaps, needed to see them, especially Thomas.

My scars aren't some kind of reminder from whence I came or part of some great testimony. I don't think about them until a nurse has to give me an IV, and I wonder if they have some way of knowing from their size that I sold blood plasma. So? What if they do?

The past really is just as it sounds, but it can have a different spelling: *p-a-s-s-e-d*. The painful parts shouldn't still cause pain, and if they do, I need to give them to God. I'm no hero for surviving things I went through. I'm not some tough guy. I'm not some faith giant. I'm just, simply, a child of God. He gets the glory; I get an eternity to witness it. Pretty fair deal, I'd say.

Blind Bart

Men share a common struggle, and the joke is, the man who says he doesn't, struggles with lying. (Guys, and probably most women too, already know what this particular essay is about.)

I had the privilege of speaking to several hundred men at a conference in Canada about this struggle and used the story of blind Bartimaeus in Mark chapter ten in preparing an address. In the story, Bartimaeus is sitting by the side of the road outside of Jericho when Jesus is coming by. "And when he heard that it was Jesus of Nazareth, he began to cry out, 'Jesus, Son of David, have mercy on me!'" (Mark 10:47 NKJV).

I like this guy. He didn't just wait patiently in line to get to Jesus. He didn't have to be sitting by the pool of Bethesda and have Jesus walk up to him. He didn't have to be up in a tree as an onlooker like Zacchaeus. No, it says he screamed out. This man had a problem and he wanted it fixed. He wasn't going to sit silent.

In an outburst to someone one day I got to that same kind of scream with "I've got something wrong with me and I don't know what it is!" Bartimaeus knew he was blind. I had no idea what my deal was. "Something wrong" was good enough for God. Jesus heard what I screamed as a prayer and two weeks later revealed to me what it was.

The struggle with sex is harder for some men than others, but to any degree, it's a problem. A man who takes a second look at another female, if he is married, is comparing that woman to his wife and indulging in lust and adultery. (Matt 5:28) A second look for a single guy is lust too. Single or married, it is not right to look upon a woman as an object for use and abuse for one's own pleasure.

Blind Bart

I toyed with the idea of entitling my message to the men in Canada "Grow a Pair" in talking about how to cope with this struggle. I shared that with the men, telling them I didn't go with it as they already had a pair, presumably. Of course, in the process, I gave away my tentative title.

There's good news in having a pair along with bad news. The good news first: what we see is what moves us men, not a bad thing depending on what we are seeing. We're mission-oriented. Women go shop for something. Men go *buy* something. It's the only logical reason I think we sent men to the moon. ("Been looking at that thing forever. Wonder what's up there?") It's also the way we approach companionship and love. We look for a woman. We find our target. We ask them out. We talk our talk. We get married. Mission accomplished. Of course, the problem for many of us is that we never talk again, but that's for another essay.

Our problem is, as American men, we're lone rangers.

The answer for me in my struggle was to find "God with skin on"—someone with whom I could break the silence, confess my struggle, open myself up to. Guess what? When men do this there's an amazing coincidence: They're going to be talking to someone with the same struggle. Duh, with a capital "D." The trick is to be the first to step up to the plate.

Back to my story of Bartimaeus: In Mark 10:49 Jesus called for Bartimaeus when he heard him crying out. Here's where something interesting happens that is all the richer if you know some history of Bartimaeus' time. It says, "And throwing aside his garment, he rose and came to Jesus" (Mark 10:50 NKJV). In that time, beggars had to wear a certain coat or cloak to identify them as such. Without it, you couldn't beg. It was like a license that a street vendor might need in today's world.

Think about throwing away the cloak for a moment. Bartimaeus didn't know what he was going to do for a living. But whatever it was, he *was* going to be able to see. The man had his priorities in order. Let me have my sight. The rest is details.

Readers, that's faith. He didn't even have to get to Jesus to get mud put in his eyes or to have hands laid on him to know that healing was coming. He knew it as soon as Jesus approached him.

I like to say Jesus wonderfully confuses me. He asks questions that not only don't make sense, to be frank, but he asks them when he already knows the answer. With Bartimaeus, Jesus asks, "What do you want me to do for you?"

"Say huh? You *do* see I'm blind, don't you?"

Jesus wants a dialogue, though. He wants to respond to our needs, but he wants us to tell him what it is.

With men and sex, guess what: Once you do cry out and tell him your need, he's going to want to keep talking to you. To put it bluntly, he wants control of our sex organs, which includes our *eye*balls, by the way, but he wants all of you . . . heart, soul, mind, spirit, and, of course, body.

Let me tell you what he's done for me. I say all the time that "my cup runs over," and I ended my first book with that. The only other way I know to explain that is to say that in terms of friends, or brothers, or relationship with Jesus, I'm the wealthiest man in the world.

I hope I made an impact on the Canadians.

I know it went in a seemingly opposite direction when I talked to several hundred men at my church's Saturday morning Bible study back home. I stood at the back of the room to talk to guys afterward, and there were two doors on either side of me leading out. You'd have thought I hadn't bathed in two weeks. It was like a Red Sea parting of those men going in two different directions, trying to keep as far away from me as possible. I understand. How are you going to come talk to me in front of your friends without them knowing why? Nope, I'm not Jesus, just a follower, but I can tell you blind Bartimaeus would have shaken his head.

Most of us know how the story ends with Bartimaeus. He gets his sight. But then there's something interesting that happens in verse fifty-two of chapter ten of Mark (NKJV) that's easy to miss. Jesus tells him to "'Go your way; your faith has made you well.'" But Bartimaeus doesn't go. It says in that same verse "he received his sight and followed Jesus on the road."

It would have been easy for Bartimaeus to go his own way—go back home and see his family for the first time; take some time seeing the sights; maybe check himself out in a mirror; figure out a job. But no, he followed Jesus.

It all began with him crying out in faith and Bartimaeus ignoring people that told him to be quiet. For us, we also have to ignore the voice of the enemy in our heads. That voice that tells us not to open up to our best friend. Or avoid that guy who just talked about lust at a men's Bible Study.

Moses, Me, and the Mount Rushmore of Anger Management

After killing an Egyptian he saw beating a fellow Hebrew, Moses receives a sharp and very telling rebuke when he interrupts a fight between two Hebrew men the next day. One of the men who saw Moses commit murder says to him in Exodus 2:14 (NKJV), "Who made you a prince and a judge over us? Do you intend to kill me as you killed the Egyptian?"

The man speaks unknowingly of Moses' future for he would become, as leader of the Hebrews, a virtual "prince and judge." But the Hebrew man also makes clear to Moses that he had no rule or reign over the violence of the two men because he didn't have rule or reign over his own violent tendencies, as evidenced by his murder of the Egyptian.

With sincerest apologies to Lofton Delgado, who I either hit or shoved into some bleachers when he accidentally whacked me on the head as he flew by me in a gym-class basketball game, I have not hit anyone in anger since the eighth grade. I have, however, had my moments that I won't share as I'd like you to continue reading without presuming I'm a madman.

I will only share that I walked around a desk to hit someone, a client of my business no less, but stopped myself before doing so. (Did I mention I once had my own business that failed? Surprise!) Not to elicit sympathy here, but I came home from this meeting and sobbed at what I had almost done.

It took Moses forty years among the Midianites on the backside of the desert to get hold of himself and even then, his anger wasn't totally stifled. In anger and frustration at the people he was leading, he strikes a rock at

Meribah in Numbers 20:11 that God commanded him to speak to. God brought forth water from the rock but punished Moses for his disobedience by not allowing him to enter the Promised Land.

It didn't take me forty years to get control of my temper but I haven't had any episodes involving walls or a windshield in a moving car in at least two decades. (Again, no details, but you probably just got the hints.) I'm not taking anything for granted, however, before I shuffle off this mortal coil, to quote Shakespeare.

I know not what follows for me, but with Moses and the murder he committed, it turned out all right. He kept his temper with Pharoah when it took ten plagues to finally convince the Egyptian ruler to free the Hebrews, and he didn't lose it when God leads him and his people out to the beach on the Red Sea and what looks like destruction or drowning.

In my case, "my time with the Midianites" was two and a half years that just seemed like forty, working with a man I would describe as difficult on steroids. I think I knew it was a test from God when I not only had to work with him but in a small room for most of that time within ten feet of him.

In an earlier life, I can state for a fact I would have invited this man to accompany me off the property where we worked for fisticuffs. Seriously.

In all truth, I may have been trying to manipulate God (only He knows if I was or not) but I resolved to be kind to this man as, again, I saw it as a test. He responded as best he could and I didn't consciously capitalize on it but went as far as telling the man on a couple of occasions I loved him and I even hugged him a time or two. I like to think I looked at him through the eyes of God and my expressions of love were genuine. He was a hurting man who wasn't all bad and who needed kindness and love. (I also needed this job and didn't want to lose it for assaulting him.)

Despite my kindness, his behavior didn't ever really change and I earned some genuine guilt by not saying goodbye when deliverance for me came through a new job.

A good five-plus years and only a few months ago at the time of this writing, I acted on that guilt, calling him to apologize for not saying goodbye when I left my job and him behind. In a certain way, it was like Moses and Pharoah after nine plagues. The Egyptian regime still held the Hebrews in captivity. With this man, he hardly acknowledged my apology and was brusque. Nothing with him had changed either. I don't know what I was

Moses, Me, and the Mount Rushmore of Anger Management

expecting, but my motive, evidently, was not pure because I regretted calling him.

I don't think of any reward for leaving anger to the point of violence behind. Maybe God will note it on the Day of Judgment as I may have spared myself and others a great deal, especially on the day this man I worked with called me a racist.

Moses *did* make it to the Promised Land, appearing to Jesus, Peter, James, and John on the Mount of Transfiguration. He paid for anger in this life, but not in the after-life with God.

I've paid dearly for anger and rage in this life, but I would like to think that like Moses, I've calmed down considerably. More important, I think I'll make it to the Promised Land.

"Let us also go . . . "

When Jesus talked of going to Judea to raise Lazarus from the dead in the Gospel of John, chapter ten, his disciples reminded him that the Jews there had sought to stone him. One disciple, however, set aside fear and spoke something with boldness that revealed a heart for Jesus perhaps like no other among the disciples: "Let us also go, that we may die with Him" (John 11:16 NKJV). Peter? James? John? No, the disciple was Thomas of "doubting fame."

Thomas was not with the other disciples when Jesus appeared after his resurrection, and much is made of his response to the news. "'Unless I see in His hands the print of the nails, and put my finger into the print of the nails, and put my hand into His side, I will not believe'" (John 20:25 NKJV).

Chiefly, the lesson we learn at Thomas's expense is that we are to have faith beyond what we can see. But if you look closely at the words uttered in the eleventh chapter of John, I think (and have heard this taught) something else was going on. Here is a man who felt that life was not worth living without Jesus in it. He was willing to die with Jesus. Make of it what you will, but no other disciple, save Thomas, was willing to do that.

With that kind of emotion and passion, I have to think the crucifixion affected Thomas differently than the other disciples. I suspect it crushed him, this earthly fate of a savior he had walked with and lived with for three years. I don't think we should be surprised that this heartbroken, devastated man would respond, in essence, "I'll believe it when I see it" when told that his savior, in whose life he had found himself, lived beyond physical death.

Think also about what Jesus did first when he appeared to the disciples a second time, but this time with Thomas there. His first order of

"Let us also go . . . "

business was to turn to Thomas and say, "'Reach your finger here and look at My hands; and reach your hand here, and put it into My side. Do not be unbelieving, but believing'" (John 20:27 NKJV). It doesn't say whether Thomas touched the wounds. He didn't have to, and I think if he did, the story would have included it. The account has Thomas simply saying "'My Lord and my God!'" (John 20:28 NKJV).

Had one of the disciples told Jesus of Thomas's reaction to the news of His resurrection? Scriptures do not tell us this, and my guess is no one had. I believe Jesus knew the toll of his crucifixion on Thomas. Just as he knew Peter would deny him three times, he knew also that the heart of Thomas—the disciple who would have died with and for his savior—needed healing and restoration to the truth of Jesus' everlasting life in those who believe. I believe the overwhelming grief in the heart of Thomas and his plaintive utterance touched the heart of Jesus. Not only did Jesus make an assurance to Thomas his priority on this visit to the disciples, but he used it to send a message to all of us today: "'Blessed are those who have not seen and yet have believed'" (John 20:29 NKJV). I don't read or see a rebuke of Thomas but a knowledge that faith without seeing would be necessary for us.

Jesus wants to assure us also of his everlasting life, particularly in times of devastation and loss. Who among us has not been in such dire straits that we haven't said, "I'll believe it when I see it"? Yet, that doesn't mean we've forsaken faith or the God who rewards it.

May we pray to see him and feel his touch as Thomas did in those times of unspeakable grief and at other times of our life. May we approach him with that same desperation and cry from our hearts to know his reality in our lives.

One last thing: Introducing the passage is something that might be easily overlooked and was most assuredly intentional on Jesus' part to show his divinity. "When it was evening of that first day of the week, the disciples were gathered together with the doors locked because they feared the Jews. Jesus came, stood among them, and said to them "'Peace be with you'" (John 20:19 NKJV). He simply appeared.

Many of us have lists of those we want to see in heaven. I want to meet Thomas. I would like to ask if he minds being known as "doubting Thomas"? I don't think he minds at all.

He was reunited with his savior in that room with the other disciples and is forever reunited with him in heaven. He is, and always will be, with a risen, living Jesus.

On the Mountain with me

Friends are the family you choose.
ANONYMOUS

" . . . there is a friend who sticks closer than a brother."
PROV 18:24 (NKJV)

Del and the Palm of God

"I have run my race; I have finished my course."

SECOND TIMOTHY 4:7

One of the perks of my ex-wife's business as a professional organizer was getting unwanted furniture from clients and sometimes more. One especially notable windfall was a top-of-the-line, king-size mattress still in factory wrapping and costing probably as much as $5,000. It would have been worth every penny had I been the purchaser, so comfortable I immediately dubbed it "The Palm of God."

Appreciation of The Palm didn't come, though, through its unbelievable comfort but an encounter with an old friend.

The main library in my city, like most in every city probably, is an escape for the homeless to get out of winter cold and summer humidity. They sit around tables murmuring to each other, killing time. If you stare too long, as is my wont, they give you that what-are-you-looking-at return stare, nominally menacing. People like small children and me are the small price for temporary comfort, I imagine.

I would not have immediately guessed the man walking in front of me one day in a library hallway was homeless. He and his clothes appeared clean, and for just a moment he looked familiar. Scars on his shaved head led me to speculate, though, he was homeless. Violence, I'm told, is common among the homeless on the streets and in shelters. Then I heard him talking to the pictures on the wall. Case closed. Try not to stare.

Preparing to check out books later, I came face to face with the man. There was a reason he looked familiar: it was Del, an art director at a marketing firm where I was a copywriter some years before. We had been friends and he was one of my favorite co-workers as he was hysterically funny.

I had seen him once before on a city bus and from that, we somehow connected on a freelance project and agreed to meet. Del had been a drug user, and I suspected something was amiss when an old man drove him to my house and waited in a car while we met to go over the project. It was the last time I had seen him before this day in the library.

His front teeth were missing and I'm sure, because of embarrassment, he explained he had lost them in a fight, and he confirmed what I suspected, that he was homeless. He told me what I'd already known, that homelessness was dangerous, and "I wouldn't believe just how dangerous."

Del falls into one of a few broad categories for the homeless: the addicted. He had blown an inheritance—$100,000, he told me—on drugs in less than a year. The talking to pictures in the hallway and some brief, odd tangents in his conversation indicated that alcohol had replaced drugs in his life.

The humor was gone but there was a genuine warmth and soft-spoken quality in his voice that wasn't there before. I had a $20 bill in my wallet and some ones, and I gave him the twenty. He didn't want to take it but said he was going to be sure and "tithe two dollars" to the lady who cleaned toilets at a shelter where he got meals.

Del had become a believer and even though there were brief moments of derangement, he was a spiritual brother now precious to me, not for his circumstances but that new warmth resting on a foundation of kindness, love, and humility.

He asked about my life and work, and I told him I had transitioned from advertising copywriting to freelance magazine work. He responded that his world had a story a writer should tell. Maybe he had in mind my sharing payment for a story or even a book. Too many writing ideas of mine are dead ends, and I didn't give it serious thought. How much trouble would it be, anyway, to connect with Del? How interesting to an editor or publisher would his nether world be? I had already failed in getting any publisher interested with a book idea on racetrack workers only a rung or two up society's ladder from the homeless.

That night I shared with my then-wife seeing Del that day as we got into our bed.

Del and the Palm of God

Sitting up on The Palm with clean sheets and under a thick, down comforter, the tragedy and sadness of someone homeless who formerly had a life of paychecks, utility bills, etc.—a normal life—were inescapable. Did Del sleep on a canvas cot or a narrow mattress on a bunk bed? Were there nights when he slept in doorways or alleys or those shelf-like spaces I've noticed on the underside of highway bridges?

Maybe it is the fear I carry around as one of the majority of us "two paychecks away from homelessness"; maybe it was the inability to help Del; maybe it was seeing a formerly funny, popular, person you were always glad to see reduced to helplessness and pitifulness, but I cried long and hard.

I was going to enjoy The Palm for a long time, but there would be many nights that I wondered where Del was sleeping.

Several years later, watching a local morning news show on television as I got ready for work, there was a story of a man who, quietly fishing with someone, had calmly gotten up from where he sat, laid his wallet and a small Bible on the ground, and dove into the water to drown himself. It was Del.

The tearless shock of Del's death wore off several hours later when relating the story to a co-worker. It was then I cried so hard and so demonstrably that he suggested with kindness that maybe I should go home. The sadness of a life ending in homelessness and then hopelessness was too heavy for my heart to bear.

I couldn't go to Del's funeral. Maybe I assumed that, because he was homeless, any eulogy would be feeble and without any real knowledge of the worth of this man. At any rate, I wanted his family to know the Del I knew, and I called the pastor officiating the service to share some things.

Instead, I heard an amazing story. The pastor told me how Del had become a ward, of sorts, of his church. He had permission to live in the concession stand of the church's ball field and to shower in a gymnasium on the grounds.

That was only the beginning. Del led a ministry of the church to the homeless that was more than remarkable. Every month, two school buses, with Del aboard the lead bus, would go into the areas of the city where the homeless lived on the streets. Del knew exactly where to go. The homeless would fill the buses and come back to the church where they would shower and shampoo their hair in preparation for haircuts for the men and boys, hair styling for the women. Everyone received free clothing and toiletries.

The ministry became a major outreach of the church and Del was the leader.

The grace of God in Del's life fills my eyes with tears several years after his death. A damaged, wounded, but ultimately precious man had found his purpose, something most of us never find.

He rests now in the real Palm of God.

"Too-Hard-to-Handle Randall"

Randy Napier, who I always addressed as "Too-Hard-to-Handle Randall," was "out-sized," to use one of my favorite terms. For starters, he had what we in the South call "Dunlop's disease," as in his belly "dun' lopped" over his belt. He had a keen wit, usually self-deprecating. His country singing was amazing and the equal of the biggest stars in Nashville. And he wore a soft heart on his sleeve. Tears came easily to his eyes.

He was a broken man in the wake of the love of his life divorcing him, but he acknowledged the fault was his. He carried this burden till his last days, but without bitterness or blame added to the load.

He also gave me something I'm ashamed to admit, which requires a brief back-story:

My particular spiritual gift, I'm told, is encouragement. I'll be your biggest cheerleader and personal motivational speaker because that's how God has hard-wired me.

It has its upside and downside, though. The upside is everybody *loves* a cheerleader. The downside is something I hate to admit, and even as I type this out, I cringe. Here it is: I will sometimes wish someone would encourage me. There I said it . . . and I don't feel any better having done so.

You might say, Billy Graham probably had his down times and needed ministry. I say this to that: I don't know this, and you don't either. I'm responsible for myself and this need for encouragement at times is mine and mine alone. To think that everyone must feel that way at times is no excuse and I'm not going to use it. All I know is self-pity, pride, selfishness, self-pity, sin nature, self-pity and characterlessness are behind this occasional need for encouragement. (Did I mention I indulge in self-pity?)

Enter Randy into my life. I'm a hillbilly from deep in the sticks of West Virginia and Randy from equally deep sticks in Eastern Kentucky. Mountains for a childhood backdrop are about all we had in common, though. Our only other common denominator was God, and when you have him in common, you don't need anything else. God brought us together through a men's fellowship and we became close.

Randy was unforgettable for a lot of reasons, but a favorite memory was him looking at me when I hadn't spoken a word and just simply saying, "Ok, let's go." He led me to the sanctuary of the church we attended down to the altar where we knelt, and he prayed for me. Boy, did I need it. This happened just twice but it meant so much to me.

A funny moment was one day when he called, and he asked me what I was doing. When I told him I was listening to a George Jones CD he understood instantly. "It's that bad, huh?"

The last time I saw him was in a hospital when he went to have his cancerous stomach removed. (I didn't know you could live without a stomach, but you can, by the way.) It was maybe the best hour-and-a-half I ever spent with any friend. I've always credited this to God, but there was not one single soul I saw the whole time in the hospital. No one at a welcome desk, no nurse checked in on him, there wasn't a roommate, and there was zero traffic in the hall outside his room. Just two very good friends talking, having some laughs, and enjoying each other's company.

I can't remember much about our conversation except for two things. One, after asking if I was squeamish (no), he showed me a photo of his stomach post-removal. The second thing is something I will carry with me the rest of my life because, without question, it was the most eloquent, shining, impactful thing I've ever heard anyone say or write. I asked Randy about his health prognosis. He simply said, "I'm going to live forever."

Wow. That sums up the believer's walk, the Gospels, a heart full of God, and the achieved mission of Jesus on this earth in five simple words. The world can't contain the totality of those few words, only the heaven where Randy does, indeed, live forever.

His life and friendship helped change my life.

My best friend today is a counselor, a kind of *guru* to both clients in his practice and others. While I give away encouragement and love, Phill gives away experience, knowledge, and wisdom. Everyone draws from him, but no one thinks to ask, How are *you* doing, Phill?

"Too-Hard-to-Handle Randall"

He has a major cross to bear that very few people know of with his adult son. I make a point to ask him about his "wild child," as he calls him, to let him know someone is thinking about him, praying for him, and that I care. Too, I have some crosses to bear with my own adult children.

The difference between Phill and me is he will never complain or whine in discouragement like yours truly is doing here.

Randy didn't complain or whine either as he lay in a hospital with a countdown begun for the remaining days and months of his earthly life.

When I got the news Randy had died, I cried and wrote on an obituary web page what Randy had said about living forever. I didn't go to his funeral and didn't feel like I needed to. I had already said my goodbyes to him. But there was a bigger reason in Randy's case.

Funerals are for the dead. Randy isn't.

Expectations and Pre-Determined Resentments

Talking to a friend, I recognized instantly he was carrying unhealthy resentments toward someone. Specifically, someone he thought was close to him didn't acknowledge his mother's death, and it hurt him. It hurt me to see my friend wounded by someone. It hurt me even more to see the quandary it put him in. He questioned the depth of what he thought was a good friendship and didn't know if and how he should respond.

I heard someone once say something unforgettable: Expectations are pre-determined resentments. Very true. My friend expected something from his friend that he didn't get. A failed expectation produced resentment.

My counsel was lame. I did recognize and tell my friend he was carrying resentment. I was weak however on the follow-through: *what* to do with that resentment.

I battle resentments myself, and you can gather from other essays what they are.

As with anything, we need to take our cue from God, and it boils down to one simple question: Does God ever have resentments toward us? No. But that's just the beginning of it.

He doesn't remove himself from us either. I thought about my friend and gave him some bad advice I need to correct: I told him to distance himself from the old friend who'd disappointed him.

Does God ever keep a distance from us? Again, no. As far as we can walk away from him, when we turn around, he is right there.

Expectations and Pre-Determined Resentments

King David provides the best example of this. Wow, what a mess this guy was. He commits adultery with Bathsheba and gets her pregnant. He concocts a plan to cover it by bringing her husband Uriah home from a battle where David assumed he'd have relations with his wife. When Uriah, out of a highly admirable sense of duty and comradeship with those he left in battle, stays outside his home, David goes to a horrendous Plan B: he instructs Uriah's commander to put him in the most dangerous battle area when he returns to war. David gets Uriah killed. Adultery and murder, by the way, were punishable by execution at the time.

There was an interesting interval in David's life recounted in First Samuel, chapters 27-29 when Saul pursued him when he went to live with the sworn enemies of God's people, the Philistines. An active relationship with God seemed to cease in this time probably as much due to physical exhaustion as spiritual despondency. But the instant he turned to God in prayer the reaction from God wasn't "And you are . . . ?" or, "So you're finally back. Took you long enough." No. Sarcasm is contempt toward someone, and God doesn't hold us in contempt. God and David began working together as they had before without missing a beat. Business as usual as David sought God's guidance.

We hear the cliché "be the better person," but does that remove resentment? No, often it ignores it without removal. The fact of the matter is, we'll dwell on the fact we're better than the person who didn't meet our expectations. That most assuredly will create a distance and will push the pride button. Pride—and it should never be forgotten—is the root of all sin.

More than that, we'll stand in judgment of the offending person. Jesus said, "'Judge not, and you shall not be judged'" (Luke 6:37 NKJV). It is almost a hackneyed cliché, worn out by believers and even non-believers. God judges, but he also does something else tied to his limitless grace and mercy. In Psalm 103:13-14 (NKJV), David wrote, "As a father pities his children, So the Lord pities those who fear him. For he knows our frame; He remembers that we are dust."

Yes, God sees what we do, but he also considers why we do it. "Frame" in Hebrew is *yatsar*, which means, "distressed" and "vexed." He knows we're born into a fallen world where distress and vexation will come through abusive parents, unfair circumstances, physical afflictions, and more. His expectations, in other words, are realistic and not subject to disappointment and resentment. Again, he knows *why* we do bad things. He doesn't judge but considers the issues we carry. And we all have them. (I joke that I have *subscriptions*.)

We're all going to disappoint someone, somewhere along the line. As a famed Bible teacher is always saying, "hurting people hurt people." I don't know why my friend's friend dissed him with his mom's death but there's a reason. That it may be a bad one—selfishness, disloyalty, shallowness—matters not. But is my friend, me, or anyone else, except Jesus, sinless? Nope. I'm an encourager and everyone likes one of those. When people start laying it on thick with me, however, I always say, hang around me long enough and I'm guaranteed to disappoint you or worse.

Back to David: If God can not only forgive an adulterer and murderer but say he's a "man after My own heart" (Acts 13:22 NKJV), what's someone not reaching out to you when you've had a death in the family? For that matter, what's *anything* anyone does? Consider three serial killers—Jeffrey Dahmer, David Berkowitz, (a.k.a. "Son of Sam"), and Ted Bundy. All came to Christ, Dahmer before a fellow inmate murdered him and Bundy before his execution. Berkowitz has recorded a powerful testimony of his salvation from his prison cell where he is serving six consecutive life sentences.

We cannot make choices for other people, but we can make choices for ourselves. They have a frame. I have a frame. (All God's chillun' got a frame. I couldn't resist.) The task is to consider it and try to act like God wants us to. To judge why someone fails us is to *be* God.

The job is already filled.

Beautiful Tears

Gary Hollow in McDowell County, West Virginia (pronounced "holler" by the natives) was a kind of unintended racial utopia when I grew up there in the 1950s. It wasn't some planned social experiment but occurred out of necessity. There were millions of tons of coal to mine—seven million annually at one time, the most of any county in America—and whether black hands or white hands mined it was of no concern. At the end of the day, everybody's hands wound up black anyway.

Integration in the coal mines was remarkable and total, and the best example might be black coal miners speaking Hungarian to communicate with immigrant foremen and other miners in the early twentieth century.

Outside the mines, blacks and whites lived pretty much together, most of us in company-built and company-owned houses. In the days of midwives instead of hospitals, my grandmother delivered my dad and some of his brothers in the home of a nearby black family.

Integration, however, wasn't total. There were two high schools, Gary District for black kids and Gary High for whites and a few blacks.

My parents taught me prejudice to be perfectly frank, as did most white parents. I will freely admit the "n-word" was part of the language with my parents and me.

I don't offer this as an excuse but as experience, and experience is never at the mercy of an argument: I and my family and others practiced what I will call cultural prejudice. It was not relational. Argue that, dispute it, judge it as you will, mount the high-horse of political correctness, but that was my experience and that of everyone around me. We white people had our biases and prejudice just as black people had theirs. But we related to each other as people, and friendships between black and white adults and children weren't unusual. If racism is hatred, then there was none.

I consider myself blessed to have always gone to integrated schools except for one brief period after my family moved to Virginia. My first day of school was the first day of racial integration at Wilcoe Grade School. What I saw that day and felt, I believe, may have had God in it because it is as fresh in my mind after sixty-plus years as it was the day after.

When I was a kid, we were eons from today's "helicopter parents." It wouldn't have been unusual for my parents and everybody else's to make sure a little first-grader got on a bus for the first time with no fanfare, no tears from mother, and no tears from the child either. I went to first grade when I was five years old (there was no kindergarten in those days) probably as much to get me out from under my mother's feet as anything. There were no worries about whether we'd be safe from kidnappers, get lost, or would run off. It's not that it was a tough environment but a different one. (I hitchhiked to the county seat five miles from my home with my neighborhood buddy every Saturday, and I think I was no older than seven or eight years old. Hard to believe, but true nonetheless.)

On my first day, I somehow knew things were different. It seemed like everybody's mom and dad came and stood in groups or alone, blacks and whites, staring and probably glaring at each other. Even as a five-year-old kid I knew there was something not just different with this picture but wrong.

Sharpening and shaping the memory was also an *absence* of difference. While blacks and whites stood separate from each other, I ran around and through them with Alphonso Wade and Larry Isom, two little black boys. They were to be my friends in grade school from that day forward, bound by football, the natural energy of little boys, and a lot of other things the three of us had in common. There was no difference except skin color.

There was also no novelty in making a friend of a different color, no high-minded intention to reach out to someone from another race. It's fake and all about the one reaching. "Hey, look at me. I have black friends. Aren't I cool?" That's patronization and racism on a different, very dishonest, and abhorrent plane just as bad as overt bigotry if not worse. The core of that crap is a search for selfish recognition: "Aren't I noble?" That exposes shallowness and a willingness to use others for selfish purposes.

We moved away when I was in middle school, and I still wonder where Alphonso and Larry are, and how their lives have turned out. Alphonso was a better-than-average football player at integrated Gary High, went on to play small-college football, and, I think, played professionally in the Canadian Football League. I don't know what happened to Larry. I remember he looked like a miniature Smokey Robinson and had a slight speed impediment that I hope went away with age. I have no memory of any other male playmates, aside from girls black and white (which wouldn't surprise a lot of people who know me well).

I thought of that day recently when my wife and I watched an incredible documentary, *Promises*. The filmmaker brought a dozen or so Palestinian and Jewish children in Jerusalem together for an afternoon. He set this up with interviews of each child individually before the gathering. Children on both sides spouted political talking points learned from parents and political leaders. One Palestinian boy, the youngest of his group, could have outdone any adult. The articulateness of his political patter was amazing and impressive enough to make you almost ignore the content.

Although Semitic cousins, there is a wall dividing the children in Jerusalem higher than that between blacks and whites in America. It goes back to ancient times and is far bigger and more powerful than concrete, barbed wire, and soldiers with machine guns that are part of life in Israel for the two peoples.

In a necessary nod to political realities in Israel, the meeting took place in a Palestinian home rather than a Jewish one. Only two Jewish children, twin boys around age eleven or twelve, out of maybe a half-dozen, crossed the boundary to meet. I give the parents of the other Jewish children, observant Jews, a pass, as I'm sure they had concerns about their children's safety. While their kids were going to a pre-determined and ostensibly safe Arab home, they would have to travel through streets perhaps not so safe.

The other remarkable thing was that of all the Jewish children, the twin boys were the only ones to come from a secular, non-observant household. Make of that what you will. There may be something there. There may not be. There probably is.

The children beautifully and profoundly replicated what happened with Alphonso, Larry, and me on that first day of grade school. They played. The joy of play obliterated the talking points, the who's-right/who's-wrong dichotomy, and the history of two peoples who are ancient brothers now estranged.

If you'd want a good cry, the emotion of a twelve-year-old Arab boy would surely bring you to it. More than the precociously articulate little

Arab boy with all the talking points (who, sadly, was the only Palestinian not to take part) this oldest of all the Palestinian children had been the angriest in talking about Israel and Jews. He spoke of hate and death to his enemies and even, if I recall correctly, martyrdom. But in that preciously dramatic emotion of an adolescent, he wept as the time neared for the group to break up. He grieved it, managing to speak haltingly through beautiful tears that he and his new Jewish friends might never see each other again. His tears were beyond words and very powerful. They were meant to express and show love to his new Hebrew friends.

It's difficult to draw conclusions from my experience as a day-one first grader and the documentary without getting into pious clichés just this side of suggesting we all join hands and sing "Kumbaya." We'd all have to stop singing at some point; continue battling our sin nature from which hate, racist or otherwise, stems; and ignore political leaders and their talking points.

Hermann Goering, one of Hitler's henchmen and one of the last persons from whom you'd expect useful revelation, explained things very simply about leading people into practically anything, including war and the slaughter of six million Jews. "It is the leaders of the country who determine . . . policy and it is always a simple matter to drag the people along . . . All you have to do is tell them they are being attacked and denounce the pacifists for lack of patriotism and exposing the country to danger. It works the same way in any country."

The key word he used is "leaders." Leaders weren't around on that playground on my first day of school or in that living room in a Palestinian home in Jerusalem.

The best question each of us must answer for ourselves is, Who is our leader? In my life, I follow a man called, among many other things, the Prince of Peace.

Thoughtful and Measured Rants on Religion

"Never forget, religion is what nailed Jesus to a cross."
KENNETH GAULT SNYDER

"Never judge Jesus by his followers."
UNKNOWN

Father Ron, the Non-Entity

I hadn't seen Ron (not his real first name) in years, and the face in the newspaper—on the front page, no less—was softer and doughier but with a different look that had nothing to do with years. There was a stricken quality, a look of this-is-what-I've-become resignation at the end of one life without assurance that another will follow. The caption told the story; it was no longer "Father Ron" but just plain Ron.

You can guess the reason for the newspaper story, and it saddens me to think of it as "the usual," but it was. There was first the "shuffle" the Catholic Church stupidly and tragically employed with Ron—the same exercise used with the many, many priests charged with sexually abusing children. The inevitable lawsuit followed that brings priesthoods ("vocations," to use church parlance) to an end and probably brings the Church a little closer to some kind of end of its own.

I converted to Catholicism but left the Church long before the scandals began. Unlike most ex-Catholics, I didn't leave after running afoul of some arcane, illogical rule made by, as one priest told me, eighty-year-old Italian Cardinals completely removed from real life. I left with respect for an institution that had hosted and birthed my own journey to find a spiritual life I had lost in my youth.

I had been friends with Ron, breaking one unenforceable church rule that you stay at your parish no matter which priest rotates in and out. When Ron left, I switched to his new assignment at a nearby parish to hear what I believe were homilies not from a file cabinet, rote formula, or seminary text, but from a soul that I believe knew God. The guy could preach, pure and simple, and preaching, as opposed to teaching, is not the norm in the

Catholic Church. And if he had that standoffishness that I've always suspected they teach priests to maintain in seminary, he stood out because of his spiritual gifts.

I knew him and liked him well enough to want to reach out to him when I saw his picture in the paper. A monster he may have been and a monster he may be now, but I didn't know him as that. I also know enough people, including myself, who have or had trouble with sex to believe it's not my decision whose sentence should be death by stoning and whose shouldn't.

I couldn't locate him through the phone book, internet, or family, and his attorney never responded to several messages I left and an email. By coincidence, I ran into a man I'd gotten to know well while a Catholic who, like Ron, I hadn't seen in years. He suggested I call his wife who had landed a job at the Chancery, the administrative office of the local diocese.

When I called her and asked if she knew how to reach Ron her answer stunned me but wouldn't necessarily surprise those sexually abused by a priest: Her exact words were Ron was "officially a nonentity." Ponder that. My iPhone dictionary app provides two brief definitions that might be the "at best" and "at worst" for a nonentity. At best, Ron was "a person of no importance." At worst, he was somebody "that does not exist or exists only in imagination." The Church can only wish both were true, particularly with that last definition.

Make no mistake, to victims' families, Ron is important, or more accurately, what happens to him is important. Ron is somebody to hate. To want to see murdered. Somebody to see at least sentenced to a long, long term in a maximum-security prison, beaten and gang-raped daily. To the victim, he damn sure exists and tragically, may exist in thoughts and emotions long after Ron is dead.

To his own family, he was probably the family star, a source of great pride and now great shame. Right now, and for the foreseeable future, I imagine Ron is a figurative rotting corpse to become a skeleton in the closet for his family. And to some of us like me, who knew him on a priest-parishioner basis, he is somebody to pity. But good God, and I do mean to a *good* God, he is, as we all are according to Biblical definition, a "sinner saved by grace." Is he now beyond God's grace? In the minds of those who choose to judge, I'm sure he is. But that's God's call, not mine or anyone else's. One thing is for certain: Ron *is*.

Father Ron, the Non-Entity

The wife of this acquaintance added, of course, that his official nonentity status prevented her from giving me his address or anything connected to him. To this day, I don't have any information about Ron.

However, I have enough about the people and the institution who labeled him a nonentity.

Pastor this or Pastor that, and How I Survived a Cult

So, what's it like to be in a cult? First of all, they're not always what you think—assemblies of zombie types or perpetually grinning loons waiting on you and the rest of the world to discover their secret. They come in all shapes and sizes, and you may find yourself in one without really knowing. Mine, for instance, was a church.

Technically speaking, by Biblical criteria, the church *wasn't* a cult, but it was within hailing distance. It functioned like one, that's for sure. The divinity of Jesus was never in question and neither was the Trinity of Father, Son, and Holy Spirit. And there was one major difference between cults and this church: Cults attract and keep followers. This church couldn't have kept members with a free turkey every Sunday. In fact, it ran through whole congregations like some churches in certain Protestant denominations run through pastors. A study of the church rolls by one of the elders revealed that every two years, 98 percent of the congregation changed. Now *that's* turnover.

I distinctly remember one individual, an airline pilot, who attended only one service, nothing unusual except for this man's background. It was in military intelligence, specifically mind control. According to this guy, what he saw and heard that day in the service was classic stuff. True story.

It's embarrassing to have been part of this church-cult, and perhaps to deflect the shame, I think back on some of the positives. I was also an elder (which adds to my embarrassment) and my time, at least, was put to good use. My wife and I visited sick people in the hospital and families in funeral homes. It was a blessing when I saw how much it meant to people and something I'll never forget.

Of course, the reason we were doing it was because *"pastor"* (never *"the* pastor" or "pastor [[name]]") wouldn't bother himself with those kinds of things. Another part of my embarrassment comes from seeing this and ignoring the gigantic red flag waving before my eyes. Here's where I found where the church ended and cult began: The foundational building block for a cult is unquestioning allegiance to the leader, and in my case, *"Pastor"* (and oh, how I hate to hear people say it without "the" in front or name behind) got a free pass from hospitals, funeral homes, and anything else remotely close to caring for and shepherding a flock. He was going to be rich and famous with no time for loving and caring for people, his flock. No profit in that.

Allegiance meant, of course, absolutely no criticism—part of control and manipulation right out of the cult handbook, if there is one. You were to never speak anything critical or negative, and even thinking a critical thought was "of the devil."

Slowly, the revolving door became evidential of something not right at this church to my wife and me. We violated the spoken and unspoken rule about criticism when it was just the two of us, and on long walks we would question things. We'd always conclude, though, that our thoughts, speculation, and talk were, you guessed it, "of the devil."

The beginning of the end for us was when the elder board began to push back with the pastor a bit. His reaction was to appoint individual assistants to us. I didn't want an assistant and expressed this but had to take her anyway. All of the assistants were women (and you can make of that what you will) and automatons who would offer no pushback and ignored their assigned elder. Essentially, they replaced us and became the elder board.

The end for me came when one family, in the two percent of which my family and I were a part, rotated out of the church. Looking back, leadership rotated just like the congregation, just at a much slower pace.

I don't think us two-percenters were more hardcore in allegiance to the quasi-cult. Instead, I think we were potential instruments of God's grace sent to help this man. I also think there were people called to this before me, and I believe people followed after me with the same mission. Towards the end of my time in this church, I had a heart-to-heart with the pastor that caused him to seriously consider stepping down and away from ministry. The gist of the meeting was me telling him he didn't care about people.

I'm still shaking my head at my departure. The pastor asked to have a final goodbye meeting but, as I quickly discerned, it was to see if I was going to be critical of the church after leaving. The selfishness and callousness of that were apparent instantly. We all say, jokingly, there is time spent at something in our life we'll never get back. In truth, that half-hour of my life was just that, and I never hear the expression without thinking instantly of this meeting.

My mind often goes to what happened to all those people who rotated through this place, and it's distressing. Did they move on to another mainstream church? I know some walked away permanently from God and religion, and that grieves me.

I sometimes wonder how I've hung in there with religion. Believe me, with the church-cult in the rearview mirror and the hundreds and hundreds churned through it, I find myself grateful that I'm still part of a body of believers. I'd say, even, I'm amazed by it.

The word "amazed" takes me to a few words from "Amazing Grace": "was lost but now I see." I'm grateful for his grace, but pray for you, dear readers, who grope through a cult or, in my case, a church-cult. May the Holy Spirit open your eyes.

And may you never have to hear someone referred to as *Pastor*.

Splash Versus Sprinkle, or the Difference between Relationship Versus Religion

I've learned there is depth and surprising reward in seemingly the most obscure passages from the Bible. (And no, I've not gotten into a study of the Book of Numbers yet but I'm expectant.) I take it on faith that if it weren't valuable and instructive it wouldn't be in there. You just have to dig a little sometimes for the value or have a great teacher to learn what even the most seemingly boring passages can teach you to change you.

With certain parts of the Bible, of course, the meaning and impact are visceral. I challenge anyone who knows the slightest about Jesus Christ to read Isaiah chapter fifty-three and not feel something deep within his or her soul, especially someone who's Jewish.

I've been fortunate to find a great teacher, and I think we all need to find someone who speaks to us individually and suits our tastes. My wife loved the late J. Vernon McGee; I could never get by the twangy, Texas accent. My teacher, outside of where I worship, is pastor of a large Calvary Chapel in Philadelphia, Joe Focht. I've listened to weeks and months in total of his hour-long teachings from Bible studies at his church. His delivery is world-weary. He always begins with a deep sigh and says what chapter from which he'll teach. No energy, just labored breathing and a low and slow baritone voice. He might take as much getting used to as J. Vernon McGee. But Joe gives me history and insight in a quantity and depth I've never heard from anyone else. And the cool part is, Calvary Chapel takes a chronological, comprehensive journey through the entire Bible Genesis 1:1

to Revelation 22:21. Nothing gets left out. You'll get the whole enchilada, and I sincerely hope I live long enough to go through every teaching by Joe on every chapter in the Bible.

Ok, to the subject at hand: Not to beat the proverbial dead horse or wear out a theme in this collection of essays, dear reader, but, in case you haven't noticed, I'm not a big fan of religion. I believe religion is necessary, but it needs to be, first and foremost, spiritual and not religious. Two "yawners" in the Book of Exodus present, I think, a dichotomy between religion and the real deal that makes the difference between spiritual and religious come alive.

In Exodus chapter twenty-eight, God gives instructions for the priestly garments Aaron and his sons are to wear. There were breastplates, ephods, robes, an embroidered coat, miter, linen breeches, and even bonnets and a girdle (?). There's even something called "ouches," basically sockets or settings for gemstones.

For me, here's where it gets good. In the twenty-ninth chapter, verse twenty-one the instruction, after Aaron and his sons have donned all the wonderful finery, is to sprinkle blood from a sacrificed ram and to make sure it's sprinkled on the garments along with the altar. Sprinkle nothing! The original word in Hebrew translates to the English word *splash*. That was inside the tabernacle. Outside, there was also a little work: "But the flesh of the bull, with its skin and offal, you shall burn with fire outside the camp" (Exod 29:14 NKJV). That's manual labor and not very desirable at that.

I love how God operates. Yep, there's beauty with the garments and I imagine the priests were pretty impressive to see. But they weren't suited up for a pageant or performance. Instead, what followed was getting down to business, or keeping the main thing the main thing: dealing with sin through sacrifices. It was messy and it stunk, and it seems like work clothes would have been better. I'd venture to say Aaron wondered, "Why do we have to get in all this finery?" And his wife probably asked, "God, do you know how hard blood stains are to get out of linen?"

The value and the instruction are partially paralleled in today's church. You have the garments for sure or worse, as in pastors in blue jeans and untucked shirts. (Don't get me started on that.) Most churches, however, forget the nasty work of confronting sin.

For many years I attended a mega-church pastored by a guy named Bob Russell who would remind you of Bob Newhart down to appearance, conservative suits, and even humor. He was probably the humblest man

Splash Versus Sprinkle

I've ever seen, which is why, I believe, God entrusted him with one of the largest churches in America. He also was a brilliant and very unassuming speaker who somehow just seemed to draw you in.

His greatest attribute, I think, was an amazing ability to lay out God's standard for living and do it in a way that convicted without offending. I don't ever remember a sermon when Bob didn't get down to the messy business of addressing sin, atoned for only by the shedding of the blood of Jesus, and dealing with the *dung* that enslaves us.

Yes, his church was a flawless hour or so of great music; brief dramas performed to the standard, really, of anything on Broadway; and truly life-changing teaching delivered with the quality you'd see from news anchors on the major networks. As if that wasn't enough, the nurseries and children's programs were models for any and all churches in America. Altogether, the church was tailor-made for folks used to drive-thru windows; things timed down to the second; articulate, polished talking heads in broadcasting; and all the other things that make us expect perfection.

Perfection, though, is what *we* want to create. *Power* is what God creates and delivers. The old hymn "There's Power in the Blood" seems archaic in today's current religious culture, but it was what God established for his people going back to the first priests, Aaron, and his sons. Life was in the blood.

The power for ultimate forgiveness was in the blood of Jesus. Order and even pageantry have their place, but it's nothing without power. "[H]aving a form of Godliness but denying its power" (2 Tim 3:5 NKJV) is what most religious worship is today. Wear the robes and even the skinny jeans to be "relevant," but just don't forget a God who parted the Red Sea, slew a giant through the hands of a kid, and finally, raised a crucified man from the dead.

Don't forget the power.

The vaccine

To equate religion to a vaccine would seem to most people natural and appropriate. After all, isn't religion and church a kind of inoculation against eternal damnation and hell? It isn't at all, according to the late Billy Graham, perhaps the greatest evangelist of our time. In fact, it can be just the opposite.

In one of his final sermons, he said that just as a vaccine is a small part of a disease injected into the body to combat the whole disease, so is religion something that can also ward off God. As a result, Graham said, religion can be the most destructive and dangerous weapon against our soul and its salvation.

Not to pick on Protestants, but how many professing Protestants of whatever stripe have a relationship with Jesus? I would imagine, taken as a whole, you're talking about a minority.

I remember well one day overhearing a conversation on the golf course that both struck and saddened me. My group and the group in front of us were waiting behind slower golfers at a tee across from a Christian school from the course. The "Christian" part of the school's name had apparently sparked a conversation. One man, in response to either a question or remark, said he attended a church then added, "Us 'middle-of-the-roaders' are a hard sell to be 'born-again.'"

The term "born-again" has become derisive and dismissive with unbelievers and, probably as a result, an uncomfortable label for believers in today's culture. It comes, of course, from Jesus' famous words to Nicodemus in the Gospel of John: "'Do not marvel that I said to you, 'You must be born again'" (John 3:7 NKJV). The use of the words speaks a great deal about

The vaccine

what it means to be a follower of Christ. He speaks to Nicodemus here of a spiritual rebirth with a different father, a heavenly Father, and a new life.

Yes, part of that newness might be church attendance, but that is only where that new life will take you. I've always said, I go to a garage every day, but I'm not going to become a car. I can go to church every Sunday and that won't make me a Christian. To be born again is to experience a second birth with a new relationship to God not just as our creator, but also as a constant, never-changing authority to whom we give honor, respect, and obedience.

It is probably no accident that it was Nicodemus, a powerful member of the Sanhedrin, which governed the Jewish sect of the Pharisees, to whom Jesus spoke these words. As a man thoroughly trained in Jewish law and theology, Nicodemus most assuredly understood adherence to Jewish rituals, feasts, and observances as part of being in right standing with God. But face to face with the Son of God—the link between man and God Himself—he knows that laws and observances—in one word, religion—are not sufficient to enter the kingdom of God.

Second Corinthians 6:18 (NKJV) says, "I will be a Father to you, And you shall be my sons and daughters." To acknowledge and know God as Father and to become a child of his does not mean our name on a church roll, regular attendance at a church, or being a proud wearer of a particular denominational label. It means to be just that, a "child," with God as a Father in whom we have fellowship and relationship. May we, like Nicodemus, set aside our church standing, our rituals, and our theology, to seek with our heart that new relationship that is the only way spoken of by Jesus to find God.

Death on the Installment Plan

"Addictions kill—relationships, careers, families, and yes, you."
ANONYMOUS

"Well, that went well."

I have been in addiction recovery for close to two decades. Addicts with a fraction of that recovery will tell you that it is easy to recognize addiction in someone else. Truly, it takes one to know one. I knew right away a woman I was dating before meeting my wife was an alcoholic.

She was staying at my home one day while I was at work, and I came home to find her under a blanket on my couch. Nothing unusual about that except she'd been under it, she told me, all day, and she wasn't sick. She'd only come out from under it long enough, so she said, to call friends to ask if she was an alcoholic. (Huh? Yeah, me too. Very strange.)

She took some kind of pride in having done this. Her question didn't baffle me and in fact, encouraged me. She knew deep down she was an alcoholic, and I knew it long before that day. The pride she took in asking friends if she was, however, had to do with everyone she'd called telling her "no," she wasn't. Denial affirmed. She asked me the same question and, because I had feelings for her at the time, I answered "yes." God says we're supposed to be "speaking the truth in love" (Eph 4:15 NKJV), and "Faithful are the wounds of a friend" (Prov 27:6 NKJV). Check. Check.

Wow, what a wound I inflicted as she instantly began screaming at me. She kept it going for maybe an hour—pure, unadulterated, high-heat, high-volume, volcanic rage. As I was a follower of Jesus, and she was an avowed, and vocal non-follower, the gist of her rage was I was a self-righteous so-and-so. Lots of so-and-sos, I recall.

I drove her home and she screamed at me the entire time on the way. She was still screaming as she opened the car door before slamming it. Don't ask me why, but I said aloud to myself as I drove away, "Well, that went well." I guess I needed comic relief. I laughed then and I still laugh now at saying that, but not at her expense.

About six months later, I got a phone call from her thanking me for being honest, wanting to repay $50 she had borrowed from me, and inviting me out to dinner on her nickel. She was clean and sober and sounded exultant.

Addicts hit a bottom that they may or may not survive. She had hit hers shortly after our scream session that was the end of our relationship for a time, and it was a close call. She had tried to kill herself with pills and had been committed to a hospital's psych ward for three days. She told me the experience had saved her life, and she soon discovered an Alcoholics Anonymous meeting in a church across an alley from her apartment building.

Maybe it had gone "well."

Looking back, in getting to know her and her life story, I saw her unbelief in a mistake made by a lot of people, confusing God with religion. In her specific case, she'd witnessed the hypocrisy of a religious family member. So, what's that have to do with God? Absolutely nothing. Yet God always gets the blame. To repeat a quote that introduced this section, never judge Jesus by his followers.

That word "mistake," has no origin pointing to some hidden meaning, but I like to think I'm on to something by breaking the word into two parts. "Mis" is to "miss" or be wrong, and a stake is something driven into the ground for support or to mark a boundary. The mi*stake* in confusing God with religion is to make a stand for a belief that *he* is religion and to drive that belief into the ground, figuratively. It is to support a position—that God is not who he says he is and, if he does exist, he is pretty much a punishing, brutal, and withholding God we should ignore or blame. Sound familiar? The withholding part is right out of the Garden of Eden and the serpent's conversation with Eve.

I've been around the proverbial horn with religion. I grew up in a Pentecostal home, somehow became a Catholic as an adult, became a charismatic Catholic, then a non-Catholic charismatic. I followed that with a decade in one of the Pentecostal denominations and then moved to a large mega-church (which is mainstream Protestantism with better music and "relevancy"). My most recent stop has been, of all things, Messianic Judaism. I joke that my next religion will be the Nation of Islam and I already

"Well, that went well."

have the bowties. (I'm Caucasian, by the way.) I've run the gamut of religions and, while blessed at all the stops, I've seen my share of things to turn me off from God. And all those things have their origin with people—*religious* people.

The Greek word for religion means to re-link or re-connect a holy God to unholy people. Notice the words "holy" and "unholy." You can't link complete purity with even the slightest particle of impurity. The only person who wasn't unholy was God's son and he is the only pure connection we can look to in life. He is the "relationship not religion" maxim in flesh, blood, action, and spirit.

Surprisingly, for an outspoken unbeliever, my friend thought the proximity of the A.A. meeting to her home was no coincidence but God's providence. In that, she saw a good God in action. I did too.

There's irony added to coincidence here: A.A. points to a Higher Power ("God" in Step Three of the Twelve Steps) with nothing religious save the Lord's Prayer at the end of some, but not all, meetings. A.A. also brings together admittedly unholy people. ("My name is . . . and I'm an alcoholic.") No hypocrisy there. And God—whether referred to as a Higher Power or the God of Abraham, Isaac, and Jacob—gets the credit for sobriety, freedom, and transformation into a new life.

Is A.A. perfect? How could it be? Just like denominational religion, it's made up of imperfect people. But God's grace overrides imperfection to deliver freedom anyway just like it can do in religion. The difference may be the honesty and accountability in A.A. There's little or no fraudulent posturing or falseness among members trying to impress others or trying to put one over on others, as in a lot of churches. And if there is, someone will probably call it out. There's also no finger-pointing at God or A.A. for failing to stay sober. If you choose to walk away from the program and the God at the center of that program, it's on you.

Oh, could it be that way with resentments toward religion . . .

May this woman find and stay with God . . . and not judge him by his followers.

"Prickly" Marty and "Pre-Marty"

I have a favorite word for difficult people: "prickly." Marty (not his real name) maybe gave the word new meaning. Firstly, he was old, which doesn't have to make you curmudgeonly (another great word), but in Marty's case, it was something he seemed to embrace. I'm within hailing distance of that age where I couldn't care less what I say or to whom I say it, so I understand. In Marty's case, what he had to say was usually in an interruption of someone accompanied by scathing disdain and correction with naked contempt. He also spoke with a raspy, gravelly voice delivered always in an "outdoor voice."

Marty was part of a recovery group of which I was a part. For him, participation was on his terms, to say the least. There was serious consideration given to asking Marty to not come to meetings.

Personality or lack thereof (except for a seemingly awful one) was only the beginning. Add atheist to the picture. That's fine in most recovery groups, but a bit of a problem where the God of Abraham, Isaac, and Jacob is the Higher Power. And we were meeting in a church in a group sanctioned by that church. So add theological differences into the mix with Marty.

I think of myself as kind. In fact, I honestly kind of like difficult people and consider them an interesting challenge. That doesn't, however, extend to recovery. I take it seriously and have no time for disruptive jerks in that arena. It's not a matter of "can't we all just get along" (to quote Rodney King of Los Angeles arrest and subsequent police-beating fame). Recovery is hard enough work without an obnoxious interloper stamping around like a

"Prickly" Marty and "Pre-Marty"

bee-stung draft horse in a flower garden. I discovered right away there were limits to my kindness. I barely tolerated Marty.

Ok, paradigm shift: It wasn't but a few weeks after Marty was in our group that he disappeared, and we all soon learned he was in the hospital dying of cancer. For any believer, an atheist in the hospital should arouse at least some concern. Taking my own spiritual temperature, I discovered I was sub-arctic and as likely to visit Marty as I was of going to the actual arctic.

A man from the group, Ralph, (also not his real name) *was* concerned. Maybe it should have been expected as Ralph was kind of a "pre-Marty." Actually, Ralph was ok . . . as long as you didn't have to do anything with him. Unfortunately, Ralph and I had a specific assignment annually on an event together for the group that required as much endurance for me as tolerance. With Ralph, nothing was going to work; everything was getting to him too late; he was never going to do this again; yada-yada. It was complaint after complaint interspersed with whines.

It floored me when I heard Ralph, without fanfare or mention to anyone in the group, visited Marty in the hospital at least twice before the old man died. Not only that, but he led Marty to a belief in God, ushering him out of this world into heaven.

Convicted is not the right word when I heard what Ralph had done; I was ashamed of myself. It showed me I was failing to "walk humbly," as the prophet Micah instructed (Mic 6:8 NKJV). Of all the men in my recovery group, the last member you would expect showed Marty God's love, care, and kindness. It affirmed that the group—whose Higher Power, again, is the God of Abraham, Isaac, and Jacob and the Father of Jesus—is truly a miraculous, deeply spiritual gathering I've always thought far superior to any church. I've referred to it many times as "my church." Something else that struck me too: God wants each of his children to find their plan and purpose.

Human nature demands we resent the laborer hired at the end of the day paid the same wage as those who had worked the entire day. (Matt 20) We instinctively measure performance. We judge, in short.

The "thief on the cross," one of the two men on a cross on either side of Jesus, was reportedly the lowest of the low as crucifixion was punishment for the vilest of criminals. Yet, the short time before his death was when his life changed, a life that didn't end in physical death but continued into paradise, according to Jesus. Did this man find his purpose in life? The immediate answer we think of is no. He played a role, though, in history, and he got a mention in the Bible, showing God's love continuing and extending to a lost soul even as Jesus, himself, was dying in agony. The thief found his purpose and God's plan for his life even as it ended.

What about Marty? It came back that his family thought he had lost his mind. I am sure he was much more of an irritant to them than he was to the guys in my group. Nevertheless, his story, if nothing else, stayed with this writer to make it into an essay. Maybe too, dear reader, it will stick with you. I hope so as you encounter the inevitable prickly people in your life or look for a purpose and some kind of plan for yourself.

In the last few weeks of his life, Marty found God's plan for his eternity. And maybe Ralph, the pre-Marty, found something within himself that will continue to grow: a purpose.

God loves prickly people, too.

"Cast the Devil Out"

My lay ministry is to addicts, and I was nonplussed by a missionary friend I greatly admire asking me why I didn't just "cast the devil out" of them. My first thought was, you can't cast someone's past out of them. Further, there's no devil *to* cast out.

Let me say upfront that I believe there is such a thing as demon possession, and I don't doubt demons have been cast out. (The movie, *The Exorcist*, was based on a true story.)

Can God not deliver addicts from their addiction? In the case of *The Exorcist*, a priest casts a demon out of a little girl.

I'd say, though, God also has a different method. My mind immediately goes to Apostle Paul asking God to remove the thorn in his flesh in Second Corinthians 2:8. God's response was "'My grace is sufficient for you'" (2 Cor 12:9 NKJV) adding, "'for My strength is made perfect in weakness.'" In short, God is saying to Paul, the thorn, whatever it was, will make you dependent on me and I will make you stronger through it. Paul went on to write the majority of the New Testament and was the greatest evangelist in history.

A look at physical healing and addiction recovery illustrates why I think God chooses to leave our thorns in place.

Surviving cancer is an event that recedes into personal history. Cancer survival will mean periodic checkups to monitor a re-occurrence. Recovery from addiction, on the other hand, is an ongoing experience with re-occurrence ready to spring at any time. Recovery requires constant vigilance, and as recovery comes from God, the addict must turn to God for continuing

FORTY DAYS

recovery. Step Three of the Twelve Steps says *we are to turn our will and our lives over to the care of God.* That means every day.

Early in recovery for me, I used to get annoyed with the "My name is (fill in the blank) and I'm an alcoholic" that must precede everything else you're going to say in A.A. meetings. What bugged me more were those who would expand on it: "My name is . . . and I'm a *grateful recovering* alcoholic." Please. Can we just get on with it? (Did I mention impatience is characteristic of an addict?) That annoyance went away over time, and my guess is I didn't have enough recovery myself to be grateful. Now I am, but still don't add, "grateful, recovering" after my name . . . yet.

I'm not "killing myself on the installment plan" anymore, which is what addiction is. I'm not living in some fog of self-absorption and borderline or even over-the-line, but invisible, insanity. Not just God but human beings are with me in loving relationships supplanting isolation. I don't live under an ever-present cloud of shame. I'm productive most of the time, not losing time to substance-inducing numbness. I don't filter thoughts through either a delusion of grandeur or an illusion of doom. I'm ok in my own skin and decent company to others most of the time. I'm not victimizing others or myself with an addiction.

Most important, I have a closer relationship with God than I ever would have had without my addiction.

Step 11 builds on Step Three in a certain sense: *Sought through prayer and meditation to improve our conscious contact with God as we understood God, praying only for knowledge of God's will for us and the power to carry that out.* There's no "until your sober and then you can stop praying and meditating" added to the instruction. It's ongoing. Step Twelve even provides a payoff: *Having had a spiritual awakening as the result of these steps, we tried to carry this message to others.*

Back to cancer and addiction: cancer survival is physical; addiction recovery is spiritual. God is in charge of both but only one of them is solely in his realm.

A cancer survivor will be grateful to doctors probably, and hopefully, God as well. A recovering addict will be grateful to God, as he or she "understood him." Chemotherapy and/or surgery will be the source of healing for the cancer survivor. The Twelve Steps and a distinct pointing to God by those Steps will be the source for addicts.

Maybe that's why, too, the Twelfth Step includes "carry this message to others." In Psalm 103:14 David wrote that God knows our *frame* (KJV), an

"Cast the Devil Out"

unusual word that, like most Hebrew, carries multiple but complementary meanings. All of us are born with a sin nature, which I always describe metaphorically as a hole in our hearts. Most of us, without God, go through life empty. Others of us—addicts—go through life filling that hole with a substance. When God says he knows our frame, he knows what we will go through and what we've been through to lead us to an addictive substance. I believe addicts are not born but created through loss, hurt, or abuse. The word frame also means purpose. He has a purpose for us, a message. God, again, has seen what has gone before us—the pain we medicated with addiction. But he also sees the purpose he would like us to find. He heals us from the wounds of the past, gives us grace for those who have hurt us, and takes us outside ourselves for the sake of others.

Deliverance or recovery? Like surgery to remove a cancerous tumor, deliverance would be a one-time experience. Recovery is every day for a lifetime.

Car Wrecks and Kisses

The last time I kissed my son on the lips was not a "Hallmark moment." First of all, he was sixteen years old and it had been a long time—longer than I can remember—since I'd done that. Second, I was mad as hell at him. He had just gotten home from running the family car into a guardrail on a wet road. He was a good driver, but he was always running late. Wet, slick roads and being in a hurry is not a good combination.

I was reading him the riot act for never leaving the house on time for wherever he was going. And then, out of the blue, I kissed him out of relief that he was ok. Joe running late was pure Joe, the laid-back kid.

It's a great memory because there was high emotion at both ends of a spectrum: anger and deep love, both expressed almost simultaneously. I still remember the look on his face: sadness mixed with distaste (literally) at his dad kissing him. It's bad enough to wreck the car and get chewed out. What a topper to be kissed on the lips by an angry dad!

I laugh about it now, and I'm sure, if he remembers it, it's not a great memory. I'm a hugely affectionate man and always was with my children, but when they're as old as sixteen, affection retreats behind certain limits.

To this day, my son invariably throws his arm around my shoulders even in public. Even better, he initiates it. I don't think to do it, mainly because he's taller and it's kind of hard for me to reach up and around him.

Joe is the first *free man* in my family line or at least the first one I can identify. Actually, he's the second, but he's the first free man from birth. I was an addict, his grandfather was an addict, and I suspect *my* grandfather was an addict. (My dad and five brothers were all alcoholics.) God bequeathed my freedom gained from the hard work of recovery from my addiction to him. Of all the benefits of recovery, raising free children is tops on the list. It's a ripple in a pond that will never cease traveling outward. But unlike a stone whose ripples diminish in size and eventually disappear, I am expecting tidal waves in my descendants.

After my son had his first child, a boy, my eyes filled with tears after his birth at the hope I have for his future. His parents will raise him in "the nurture and admonition of the Lord" (Eph 6:4 KJV), and increasingly in this world, that is a rare thing. My recovery was all about "my own boys"—my son and now my grandson. I have no idea what Anderson will grow up to be, but I have all the reason in this world and the spirit realm outside it to expect him to be a great man.

Visiting the little guy a few days after his birth, I laid hands on his little head and prayed for him as my son held him and his mom and grandmother stood nearby. I thanked God that his parents will raise him as he should be. I also thanked God for a will, a plan, and a purpose for his life.

It is an awe-inspiring thought to think that God knew Anderson before time began, that he saw him coming into this world to the parents and grandparents God planned for him.

Unfortunately, today this sounds like a fairy tale, even to probably most who call themselves Christians. But here's what the Bible says: "I chose you before I formed you in the womb; I set you apart before you were born" (Jer 1:5 CSB). "[H]e chose us in him, *before the foundation of the world*" (Eph 1:4 CSB). That latter verse seems inconceivable to the human mind, yet it is truth.

The tendency is to look at our own lives and see family dysfunction, lives in sin, years and even decades of distance from God . . . and we don't see where God has brought us. More egregious, we don't look at following generations at how far ahead they are through what God has done in daddy or grandpa.

He brought me along after, oh, fifty years (!) of desert wandering, to put it euphemistically, (or "dessert wandering" through things I don't want to go into here). The point is, he brought me through, just like he did his people after bondage in Egypt, Joseph after his sale into slavery and imprisonment in Egypt, Moses after committing murder, and on and on.

David is, with Joseph, my co-favorite of all the bound-but-set-free types in the Bible because he was so flawed in so many ways—a horrible father, a philandering husband, and last, a premeditated murderer. Yet he made it, becoming a man "after God's own heart," and his descendants eventually included Jesus.

I loaded a bin of things from my life to take to my son's house—media passes from sports events I'd covered as a writer, things from my dad, odds and ends from my life. These things are not so much for Joe as for my grandson, Anderson. I want him to know who his "Papí" was after I'm gone, but what I really want him to know is the God that changed me. His parents, I'm confident, will take care of that.

As for me, he may not know it, but he will walk in the good work God began in me almost twenty years before his birth.

Two Steps

To describe working through the Twelves Steps of addiction recovery I always say it is really just two steps: Step One: stop using whatever you're using; Step Two: change everything else about your life.

It always gets a laugh when I share it with others, but there's a lot of truth in this. I've had to pursue changing everything about my life, a pursuit that will be lifelong, to keep me from using what I was addicted to.

For the most severe sufferers of alcohol or drugs, the first step can be jail or involuntary rehab. An unforgettable story for me is that of a bank vice-president I know sitting drunk and hand-cuffed in urine-soaked pants in the back of a police cruiser and hearing audibly the voice of God: "Frank, do I have your attention?" The handcuffs and a night in jail took care of the physical part of recovery, at least temporarily. Frank had no choice in the matter. Hearing God gave him a choice, and life, as my wife says often, is all about choices.

Whether locked up or coming to the end of yourself on your own, it's a lot easier to stop a behavior than to change everything else about your life. The problem is, if you don't change everything else about your life, you'll go back to the behavior. I saw something early in recovery that I've repeated many, many times to addicts: the answer is easy, but the solution is hard.

Here's a secret, though: It's God who does the changing. In fact, two real steps from the Twelve Steps address this: Step Two: *Came to believe that a Power greater than ourselves could restore us to sanity.* Step Three: *Made a decision to turn our will and our lives over to the care of God as we understood Him.* Paraphrased, this says you can't do it without God, and you can't do it without putting it all—everything—in God's good hands. The *Big*

Book of Alcoholics Anonymous says, "Half measures availed us nothing." Those are five incredibly powerful words if they're followed.

Addicts learn that sobriety and recovery are not synonymous. You start with sobriety and if you work hard enough; and want it bad enough; and if you're patient with yourself; and if you're willing to bleed, sweat, and cry; and if you can lay yourself out on a figurative cross and let nail-drivers pound away, you'll get recovery. It will change your life, and it will be a far better one than you could have imagined.

Step One—*We admitted we were powerless over our addiction—that our lives had become unmanageable*—is to acknowledge the problem. Addicts are the world's best liars, honing it from a skill into an art to preserve and protect themselves and the addiction they hold onto. Addicts, however, don't just lie to everyone around them but to themselves. To stop lying to yourself is the beginning of a journey to freedom.

You can't get to God unless you first admit you can't do anything about your problem and ask him for help. If this isn't the most beautiful step (and I can think of no other word but "beautiful" for it), it is the only one that some recovering addicts believe you're guaranteed to do perfectly.

I've been a believer most of my life, but when I hear the hymn "Just as I Am," which always accompanied the great Billy Graham's altar calls, it brings tears to my eyes. We come to God a wreck, but there's no right or wrong way to come to God except to come just as you are. We humans are all wrong and we will never be right until we leave this fallen world.

One of my closest friends and first sponsor in recovery is a character, and I will frequently say to him, "Phill, you ain't right" to which he always replies, "I know, but I know somebody who is," meaning, of course, Jesus. We come to God as imperfect, flawed persons, but he doesn't care because his love is perfect towards us. The choice to come to him, despite all our failings and flaws, is a perfect one.

This essay had to be in this collection among all the others because the Twelve Steps (or Two Steps) took me to the mountaintop and God. God, again, wants our all, and "half measures" don't cut it. That means all the way to the mountaintop and not halfway up.

Moses had to go atop a mountain alone to be with God for forty days. Abraham had to take Isaac to the top of the mountain to sacrifice him before God provided a ram in the thicket.

A mountaintop is a lonely place but a necessary one to hear from God. What has been my experience? Firstly, I came to realize it's not me who

Two Steps

changed my life but God. This loses everything in translation and I even struggle with the depth of it myself, but I recently heard my favorite Bible teacher say there's no such thing as "my recovery." It is *God's recovery* and belongs to him.

Heck, I can't even take credit for choosing to pursue recovery. He first loved me. He ordered my footsteps because I became his righteousness. He ordained me for good works. He did it all.

I think of his last words on this earth: "It is finished." Nothing more to add to that . . . it *was* finished. It really is a couple of steps toward God that isn't effort but choice.

Despising the Shame

For basically the first fifty years of my life, I lived in shame. I did things in secret that made me two persons—a believer who devoutly pursued and loved God and an addict who loved something more than God—an idol obstructing the fullness of God that made me a slave. Oh, I was popular and entertaining (Class Clown in my high school graduating class), but it was a cover for deep, consuming insecurity. The only time I was real, in truth, may have been in my idol worship. I was a slave, yes, but in a strange way, I was acknowledging inner pain and shame. In those hours when I was indulging my addictive substance, I was medicating what I felt and believed about myself. I hurt, and that was my reality.

The very first consequence of the fall of Adam and Eve was shame. After eating the forbidden fruit, they immediately sensed their nakedness and covered themselves. What happened? Why did they suddenly feel shame about nakedness that had been natural and something of which they had been unaware before that moment? The reason is simple: they had, with one act of disobedience, left a state of total God-consciousness for self-consciousness. They used fig leaves to cover not only nakedness but also shame. Satan's promise that the fruit would cause them to be like God was a lie. They could not think of themselves as the same person before God that they had been. They were, to a degree with which we all deal, separated from God.

We get the same lie every day in our lives. Television commercials selling beer subconsciously promise us acceptance and even sex if we drink a particular brand. The promise belies the broken homes, hopeless alcoholism, or highway fatalities that are often very real consequences of drinking

Despising the Shame

for some of us. On another level, a potential affair promises us emotional fulfillment and love when guilt, shame, shattered lives—*separation from God*—are the real results.

Our sin, rather than delivering a promise, produces shame just like it did with Adam and Eve in the Garden of Eden. And just as Adam and Eve covered themselves with the fig leaves, we cover ourselves, retreating behind what psychologists call a *persona* that is not really us.

A Catholic priest and psychologist, who has written about the subject of shame, describes it as something that puts us "beside ourselves." We don't think of ourselves as we should because we are not *in* ourselves or in our right minds.

Jesus went to the cross "despising the shame." The word "despising" would make you think he experienced an emotional revulsion at his crucifixion—that he hated the shame of the cross. The original Greek translation, however, provides a surprising definition. The word despising means, "to think against." He was not a criminal. He was, instead, the Son of God, and his journey to those nails, a crown of thorns, those pieces of wood, and those agonizing hours demanded an incredible will and an inestimable strength of mind. He had to know and believe who he was to endure the physical and emotional ordeal of the cross. Think, too, for the first time in his eternal life, he experienced separation from his Father, all the while thinking against that separation, remembering he *was* the Son of God.

The lesson we as Christians can take from Jesus "thinking against" the shame is that we are not what we think we are or what the world may think of us in our failings. The devil is an "accuser of our brethren" (Rev 12:10 NKJV), quick to condemn us for our sins and to make us feel like we neither measure up to others around us or to a standard that God has for us. In short, he is quick to make us feel ashamed.

But just as there was an empty tomb and a resurrection for Jesus, there is also for us a spiritual resurrection through God. In and through God we can rise above the accusations of the enemy and the shame he wants us to feel.

The Apostle Paul instructs that you are to be "transformed by the renewing of your mind" (Rom 12:2 NKJV). Jesus steeled his mind to take on the pain of the cross and the shame that would come with it, and we can transform and steel our minds with what God says about us throughout his word. Here is a brief but powerful sampling of some of those things: We are "the righteousness of God" (2 Cor 5:21 NKJV); members of a "royal priesthood" (1 Pet 2:9 NKJV); "My sons and daughters, Says the Lord Almighty" (2 Cor 6:18 NKJV).

The fall of Adam and Eve did indeed produce a break between God and man restored through Jesus and the blood he shed on a cross. But did God love Adam and Eve, his creations, any less after their fall? No, of course not. He loved them so much that he sent his only son to die for all that would be born into a fallen state not reconciled to God. Does he love us any less when we fall for lies and are disobedient? As Christians, we know he forgives and that his mercy is never-ending.

Acceptance of his forgiveness and reconciliation with God also means something maybe more important than anything else: we can stand before him and others without shame.

Faith and Other Adventures in Desperation

"One breath, one heartbeat follows another.
You may as well have hope because you can't stop either."
ANONYMOUS

"Without faith, it is impossible to please God.
Life's unpleasant enough on its own to go through life without it."
UNKNOWN

The Desire of our Heart and What to Desire

I am in my sixties and never struggled with the major age milestones . . . until I hit sixty. My daddy died several years before that. (For all you readers outside the South, it's "daddy" and never "dad," no matter how old you are. I'll go back to "Yankee-ese" in the other essays.) His five brothers were like him, all dead from heart disease in their mid-fifties.

I couldn't help but think, "I'm pushing it." It took about six months to get comfortable with my age (and somewhat comfortable with the thought I could drop dead of a heart attack at any moment). No, I'm not a heavy smoker (although I was as a young man), or an alcoholic, something my dad, and all my uncles were to a person.

I learned in the time leading up to my daddy's death something about a familiar scripture: "he will give you your heart's desires" (Ps 37:4 CSB). The scripture has two meanings, one of which most of us overlook or do not ever see at all: God will show us *what* to desire.

It never occurred to me, as I watched my daddy weaken and head toward death, to ask God to give him a miracle and deliver him from heart disease. Did I *desire* to see him live? That's not an easy question to answer.

I discovered after his death he was committing slow suicide in the wake of my mother's suicide. He even admitted this to my sister. Although divorced and remarried, my mother was the love of his life and her death broke his heart. He had gone back to alcohol even before their divorce and took up smoking like a proverbial chimney. Before that, the "family curse" had already begun with the old nitroglycerin pills for a failing heart and then triple-bypass surgery that gave him a few more years of life.

Call me lacking in faith. Whatever. It just never occurred to me to pray for a miracle, and while I battle guilt with a lot of things, I don't feel guilty about not praying for this.

What I did pray for was something that saddened me: Despite what I believe was an absolute death wish, I found out he feared death. This was something I became aware of a few months before it happened. That brought me to my knees in prayer. I had no problem praying for this, and I believe it was a desire that God gave me.

It was around three weeks before he died that God answered my prayer. Daddy's heart had deteriorated to a point where the muscle just briefly stopped one day. I know it was God that had him experience this and to tell me about it. He told me that as he was falling to the floor, he knew exactly what was happening... and it felt wonderful, he said, beyond any worldly experience. He felt a peace he had never known. The colors of all the things around him became more vibrant and beautiful. And his fall was in slow motion and gentle with no concern for impact with the floor. After all, he was dying, and he knew it. To quote Apostle Paul, death had no sting. Prayer answered. He had no fear of death from that point on.

He went into the hospital at some point shortly after that for the last couple of weeks of his life. I lived in a city seventy miles away from his and found myself in my car many days after work driving to see him. It was completely without thought; I'd find myself driving that way and not home. I went to see him the same way I had when I lived in the same city as him, visiting not out of obligation but some unconscious force that still baffles and blesses me.

We had a poor relationship when I was growing up, but it changed when I became an adult, and I'm sure it was God's restoration. The last few years of his life were the best years I ever had with him.

He is a difficult man to describe and just plain difficult in his own right. One of the million and one quirks was this outspoken, defiant preference for one thing over another. The problem was, there was no need for a preference with most, if not all, of those things. To wit, the Old Testament with daddy was far, far better than the New Testament. He would argue with anyone about that. Hey daddy, they're both good—Old Testament revealed in the New, the New concealed in the Old. Nope. The Old Testament was far, far better, according to him.

This odd argumentativeness over preferences would baffle Freud, but I know he lived a tormented life, a son rejected by his mother, and brother to five siblings, all of them accepted and loved by her. The result was a walk with God tragically hampered, a walk with what I call a "spiritual limp." But he walked, nonetheless. He studied the Bible diligently (both the Old and New Testaments, ironically). And each night we all had to be quiet in our small home as he prayed for more than a few minutes on his knees next to his bed before sleep.

The limp came from the pain of his rejection and subsequent enslavement to alcohol to medicate that pain. Making it worse, he *didn't* drink for many years but lived with a craving that made him irritable, discontented, and restless, the classic description of those who struggle with alcohol. He went to one Alcoholics Anonymous meeting and sadly, very sadly, pronounced himself cured. He never got to the root of why alcohol consumed him mentally and spiritually, if not actively. He limped along with God as if tethered to the proverbial ball and chain, following as best he could and even keeping up, but chafed, chapped, and bleeding. He had one foot solidly in the kingdom and the other dragging along this burden. God rest his precious, tormented soul.

I think the Holy Spirit knew I both marveled at his defiant, argumentative preference for one thing over another and knew what I, a loving son, needed. As I left his hospital room one evening, he raised himself from his bed to poke his head around the corner to see me in the doorway. His parting words were, "I've been studying my New Testament." It was the last thing he ever said to me and I never saw him alive again.

Oh, my God is good. He removed daddy's fear of death and more. He gave him perfect love far, far beyond mere acceptance or the love a mother could have given him. And God assured me, with those few words my daddy said, that he gave him a home in heaven . . . one I won't have to drive to.

Hope Images and Horsepower

I have a confession to make that may stop some of you from reading if you are of certain denominational persuasions. I was a follower of the "Word of Faith" movement, big in the 1980s and nineties. You know. Name-it-and-claim-it.

And here's where I really may lose you: I will contend there were "babies in the bath water" of Word of Faith that I've been careful not to throw out. One is a scriptural principle the Word of Faith homed in on easily overlooked and perhaps perplexing to some mainline Protestant folks.

I learned and applied this principle from the Old Testament story in Genesis 30 of Jacob dividing a herd of sheep with his father-in-law, Laban. Jacob agreed to take the spotted goats and sheep (less valuable and desirable than solid-coated) and Laban could have the rest. Good deal for Laban, right? Not so fast. Jacob's name in Hebrew means "supplanter," or someone who schemes to replace one thing with another. Like a lot of instances in Jacob's life, he lived up to his name.

Jacob took branches or rods and cut speckles into the bark before laying them into the watering troughs of only the strongest and best of the spotted animals. Somehow, someway, it put before the moms and dads of future sheep an image that translated into, you guessed it, spotted, speckled and strong offspring. For the solid-coated weaklings of the flock, he put no branches in the troughs. "Sorry about your luck, Laban. I have no idea why my sheep turned out great and yours didn't." Never make a deal with someone whose name means supplanter.

Hope Images and Horsepower

The principle is to put something before you that you want, a hope image. The ever-crafty Jacob put before the sheep something *he* wanted, and they had no say-so in the matter.

At one time, as I've written about elsewhere in this collection, I didn't have a receptacle for urogenital excretions or an aperture for disposal, to express it euphemistically. (If you don't get it, I explain it later.) Part of my poverty was not having a car or not much of one.

What I also didn't have was "works" to go along with faith—"faith without works is dead" (Jas 2:26 CSB). More specifically, I didn't have enough "work" to afford a car. But what I did have was the story of Jacob and his speckled rods and faith. And what I needed was a hope image—a figurative speckled rod to put before me.

My then-wife was also Word of Faith and agreed to my idea of going and looking for a car as if we had money to buy one. She wasn't too keen on what I settled on for a car brand, but that's an important part of the story I'll get to later.

I had no idea that test drives can span more than a drive around the block but an entire weekend, at least with the dealer we visited. I enjoyed the car that I liked the whole weekend with nary a thought that I'd have to return it Sunday evening. My wife and kids were mostly silent as they weren't crazy about the car. (As my father used to say, there's no accounting for taste).

The moment is one I'll never forget. About a month after our test-drive weekend my wife called me to matter-of-factly announce, "Judge wants to buy us a car." The judge was a client of her business and a kind, good, and also wealthy man. This kind of generosity, however, was unprecedented.

Honestly, it didn't shock me. I believe hope is the steppingstone to faith and faith rewarded. I had built hope by driving a vision for what I wanted, applied faith to it, and, through my wife's client, God gave us a car out of the clouds . . . literally.

There was no short-changing God, either. We were getting a *new* car. Armed with a check for $20,000 (this was maybe twenty years ago when $20k would buy you a nice new car), we drove to a dealer that had the car to satisfy everyone's taste and drove it home.

I defy anyone to tell me hope images are bunk and Jacob's speckled rods are just an interesting story of horticulture and animal husbandry. The blind man with sight restored responded to interrogation and disbelief with

"One thing I know: that though I was blind, now I see" (John 9:25 NKJV). I test drove a car with no money, acting on faith with nothing more than a hope image, and a man decided a few weeks later to buy my family a brand-new car. Disbelieve all you want. All I know is, once I didn't have a new car, and now I had one.

Fast forward ten years to when I was, once again, absent a pot and a window (see "receptacle," "aperture" etc. above) in the wake of a divorce. I had a car, but not one trustworthy enough for a somewhat long commute over one-hundred miles round-trip daily for a new job. Here's where a more familiar faith story came into play: Peter's walk on the water. With no money for a down payment, I stepped out in faith, so to speak, and went to a dealer anyway.

It had been a while since I'd *bought* a car, so it shocked me when the salesman pointed to my old beater and said, "There's your down payment."

The story gets richer when that dealer didn't have what I was looking for on the lot. I went to another dealer with the same car brand. I wanted a white car. I wanted a manual transmission or stick shift. And I wanted the larger of two engines available with this model that had more horsepower.

All I specified with this second dealer, however, was the manual transmission. He called someone to drive up what they had on the lot with a stick shift. When driven up to the showroom door you can guess the color: white. I was so excited I forgot to check the engine size until several days later. You guessed it again: it had the larger, higher horsepower engine I wanted.

One other thing that also shouldn't be a surprise: it was the same car make that I had for my test-drive weekend. Whoever said the devil is in the details had it wrong. *God* is in the details . . . and in hope images.

All coincidence? That's probably what Jacob told Laban.

"Hey God, would you mind holding my coat for a 'sec'?"

Faced with a situation where I felt I needed counsel, I, as any believer probably should do, sought a Christian counselor and not a secular practitioner. I left a counseling session with solid concrete advice and even step-by-step answers on how to approach my situation. But I also left feeling frustrated and disappointed with one nagging question still in my mind: But what about God?

Much of that question came from a familiar pattern in my life: I didn't seek God first through prayer and meditation.

Did I receive good counsel? Certainly. But in not going to God first, I had forgotten the scripture and the assurance within it, "casting all your cares on him because he cares about you" (1 Pet 5:7 CSB). And, of course, why I didn't go to God was a complete lack of faith in hearing from God for that step-by-step answer to my situation. (Gulp. There I said it, and may God forgive me.)

In relating the situation and the dissatisfaction to a friend, he expressed most eloquently my frustration in just a few words: "You're asking God to hold your coat while you go to work solving your problem." A counselor and I were going to tackle this and God holding my coat wasn't even an afterthought.

Most Christians believe the words "God helps those who help themselves" are biblical. The author, however, is not an Old Testament prophet or a New Testament apostle, but instead, Benjamin Franklin. The words, of course, aren't in the Bible.

Franklin didn't have it all wrong. To ask God for a job and not write a resume and look for a job is not helping yourself. But there are many times where we cannot help ourselves. The Serenity Prayer beautifully asks God to grant the serenity *to accept the things we cannot change; courage to change the things we can; and the wisdom to know the difference.*

Yes, there are things we cannot change that require acceptance. But those are also what God looks at and says, "No, you can't change this. But I can."

In my situation, I felt I needed someone else for counsel. But that wasn't God, the God who does indeed care for all things and whose Word encourages us to bring him all our problems both large and small.

We all need to do our best and do what we can do. But we also need to remember that Moses' "best," as leader of God's people, was to bring them to a beach on the Red Sea where they were either going to drown or suffer slaughter at the hands of the pursuing Egyptian army. Moses couldn't change the geography of the situation, but God could. When Moses had nowhere to turn but to God, he and the people received a miracle.

I'm reminded of a worship song popular some years ago taken from Psalm 60. Perhaps he was giving us words we should never forget when facing any trial, situation, or circumstance in which our best isn't good enough. (italics added below)

"*Through God*, we shall do valiantly:

For *he it is* that shall tread down our enemies."

(Ps 60:12 KJV)

May we remember that God doesn't want to "hold our coat" while we go to work on a problem or situation. He desires to take off his own coat and go to work on our behalf.

Manna and Better Days

Someone has figured out that forty tons of manna had to fall every day from the sky to feed the two million Hebrews in the Sinai wilderness as they made their way to the Promised Land. In one regard, that might be a miracle greater than the parting of the Red Sea. This was *daily* with even a double portion to fall on the day before the Sabbath when it did not fall to not interfere with a day of rest.

Yet, this stiff-necked people, as God described them, insisted on a golden calf for a God, grumbled and complained, and drove God to serious consideration of wiping them out. The monstrosity in spiritual and literal blindness is beyond words. "Oh, taste and see that the Lord is good" (Ps 34:8 NKJV) was literal.

Yet, I have been that same person.

I've eaten my share of manna in my life and been just as ungrateful as the Hebrews coming out of Egypt.

I've been everything short of homeless and was sure that would happen. Here's how bad "my wilderness" was emotionally: I've composed suicide notes in my head and figured out how to do it to not scar my son if he found my body. And I've frightened an experienced counselor with one bout of depression.

Maybe the only difference between the Hebrews and me is I wasn't ever a slave. And the fact of the matter is, I *was*. (That's for another time and another book.) I wrote about "my wilderness" in another essay herein ("Joseph's Sentence...") and the sordid details are there. What I've left unwritten for this essay, though, was the manna that God provided.

Forty Days

First of all, let me say I think we might be a little hard on God's people for their idol-building and disobedience. Consider their life out there: Yes, there was manna from heaven. But there were also extreme temperatures in an austere environment. (The term "God forsaken" comes to mind, as I'm sure it did theirs). They didn't know when they were going next and where. There were long periods of idleness. The only relief was moving, and who likes to pack and move, especially when the new destination is likely to be no different from the one you just left. Last, but not least, it was for forty years!

My own "manna" was miracles of provision both large and small that always arrived at the brink of what would have been a disaster for my family and me.

I was on the verge of losing my home when I had lunch with a friend who told me he felt led to give me "mad money" he carried in his wallet. It was a substantial sum and paid my mortgage. (He must have planned on his wife being *really* mad.) He was completely unaware of my financial circumstance by the way.

On another occasion, it appeared as if my wife at the time and I were going to have to pull our children out of a Christian school. Foolish or not (given how much of a financial struggle it was to keep them there), God made a way. I felt a bulge in a jacket pocket one day where someone had placed another substantial sum. It caught me up on tuition. Again, whoever put it there did not know the circumstance we were facing.

The incidences I just recounted (and there were more than I can remember), were provisions to make it another day. But another day like the last one was nothing to look forward to. I wanted a good job like the ones I had had. Yet, I had what I needed: manna.

The turnaround began when I got an email one day from an old acquaintance asking if I was interested in a technical writing job. I'm surprised he remembered me, but I remembered him well for an odd reason. My wife at the time and I had visited with him and his wife years back to help them save their marriage. What I recall was puzzlement over how we wound up doing this, driving some twisting county roads in rural Kentucky one Saturday. I never did get the straight story on how the meeting came about. Looking back, I would say with some certainty that I was sewing a seed for a future harvest—the job the man offered me.

Manna and Better Days

The job paid a respectable salary and led to another position with a Fortune 500 company. I was, however, laid off in a third wave of massive layoffs with this company.

I had been remarried not quite a year when the layoff occurred, and my new wife and I had enough to sustain us but only for six months or so. I'm embarrassed to admit I took unemployment but have to share this, as it is instrumental in what happened. The day I cashed my last unemployment check was the day I got a job offer for another job at a salary almost 70 percent higher than what I was expecting or would have taken.

Obviously, I've lived a life of extremes. The important thing, though, is I've seen God in that life whether it was daily provision or a turnaround.

Manna will get you to the next day and, just like the Hebrews, one of those next days will be the beginning of better days.

Post-It Notes and Other Trophies

I carry a Post-It note in my wallet that is a trophy in my walk with God.

I've regretted not keeping prior trophies, specifically, a copy of a check I received from an employer many years ago (and there are more things I wish I'd kept). The origin of this Post-It was a proposal in my job that, had my company lost, would have meant hundreds of persons packing boxes to find employment elsewhere. Me too, I might add.

The day that produced the Post-It note began in the darkness of an early Sunday morning well before dawn on a drive to my office. Sunday wasn't abnormal as I think I worked twenty-one days straight on this proposal, but the early hour was unusual. There was a major gap in the proposal that I needed to fill, and the document was going out that evening. The drive was more prayer than driving, as I needed God to give me an answer as to what the "fill" would be. I had no idea.

God was and is faithful, and he gave me what I needed. The Post-It note carries something I've forgotten that was part of what God gave me for the proposal. I felt I very much needed to keep it as a trophy. That's not the end of the story, though.

We lost the competition for the contract.

I was shocked and immediately went into panic mode as to my future with the company and that of many, many co-workers. Immediately, I thought of the Post-It note in my wallet, thinking I should throw it away.

Something told me to hang on to it, however, for reasons I couldn't explain.

Post-It Notes and Other Trophies

It's a stretch, maybe, to link the Post-It note to a man named Jairus whose daughter was dying in the Gospel of Luke. I make the connection because a sermon I heard on Jairus was one of the best I've ever heard and because there was a great lesson in it that I recalled with the Post-It note episode. To recap the story, Jairus is desperate, so desperate he walks to the Sea of Galilee in hopes of encountering Jesus. That's "in hopes" as there was no commercial ferry with a timetable and no way of knowing exactly when or where Jesus would land. Jesus does arrive, though, and Jairus falls at his feet imploring him to come to his house for his dying daughter. So far so good.

But not for long.

Crowds thronged Jesus, including a woman with the issue of blood who touched the hem of Jesus' garment. In the sermon I heard, the preacher believed, as I do, that Jairus was in a quiet panic, asking to himself if not to Jesus, "Can we just get on with it?" Jairus is probably frantic and is then devastated when someone from the synagogue of which he was a ruler comes to tell him his daughter is dead.

Jesus spoke to Jairus, saying, "'Don't be afraid. Only believe, and she will be saved'" (Luke 8:50 CSB).

We all know the story from there. Jesus comes to Jairus' home and gets ridiculed because the little girl is dead. He throws everyone in the house out, which probably included the messenger bringing news of his daughter's death to Jairus, and entered the home with Peter, James, John, Jairus, and the girl's mother. Jesus resurrects her—"Her spirit returned" (Luke 8:55 CSB).

With my proposal, there was a protest of the award, almost routine for contracts with the Government the size of the one for which we competed and typically denied. I maintained hope because of the Post-It note and what I believed was God telling me to hang on to it, but I didn't think much about the protest either. Like I said, more often than not, protests don't succeed in overturning an award.

Months later my boss and a co-worker on the proposal came into the room where I was working and told me that not only was the protest upheld but our company won the contract.

I'm not vocal or demonstrative in my faith and walk with God, but I threw my arms into the air and loudly said, "Praise God!" before these two people.

I still have that Post-It note and will probably always carry it with me. (And for the life of me, I can't remember the meaning of the notes I made on it that directed me in the document.)

The lesson for me is never, like Jairus, take bad news as the final word. Losing a job and others losing theirs because of a losing proposal competition is not as awful as losing a child. But a loss is still a loss.

You don't lose, like Jairus and I learned, when God tells you it's not over and to have faith. One thing of note is that the scripture passage doesn't give any response from Jairus to the messenger or to what Jesus said when he received the news that his daughter was dead. Jesus doesn't respond to the messenger either, but ministers to Jairus. Jairus, even with the news, maintained his faith in Jesus. Maybe he was like me not discarding the Post-It note; there's something to hang on to. In my case, it was a small piece of paper. In Jairus' case, it was Jesus standing with him on a road to his home.

God decides and we accept his decisions. But we wait on *his* decision sometimes written on tablets of stone, sometimes in the life of a twelve-year-old girl, and sometimes on a Post-It note in a believer's wallet.

God the Golfing Partner (yes, God!)

Some years ago, I received a miracle unbelievable in more ways than one. No, it didn't involve some kind of healing or financial windfall. Instead, it was something so obscure and seemingly insignificant that it probably requires more belief than if I had the kind of miracles just mentioned. In fact, if I related it to you personally, you'd probably smile politely and maybe stammer out in befuddled and embarrassed amazement, "Really? That's nice." The "that" I'm writing about is, of all things (gulp, blush), golf. Yes, golf.

As a new, excited, and enthusiastic believer who had come back to God after many years' absence, I took literally to heart the scripture that says we should be "casting all your care upon Him, for He cares for you" (1 Pet 5:7 NKJV). With simple, childlike, and what some would say ridiculous faith, I deduced that since the scripture didn't say cares for all things *except your golf game*, then this verse covered it. Never mind that there was no golf at the time of this scripture's writing. (Details, details . . .)

First some background: I'll never forget a question that somehow came up in conversation with some golfers one day: Who invented golf, God or the devil? Now if you're a golfer and a believer, that's a great question and a head-scratcher. The answer is a bored Scottish shepherd whacking a rock or something around who had a light-bulb moment when it rolled into a hole. Maybe the better question is, Who inspired this shepherd? God or the devil?

Put me firmly in the devil camp. Golf, for me, is maddening, not just for me but for others. I've seen a scratch golfer go ballistic at one or two bogeys in his round of golf. I've also seen a golfer throw his golf bag into a lake, forgetting, on his stomp back to the parking lot, that his car keys were in the bag—still one of the best laughs I've ever had. Thrown clubs are not out of the ordinary at all, and I've broken a club doing that very thing.

Living in my skin, living with my issues, golf was a source of actual depression. (It's complicated.)

Golf will get to you for any number of reasons one discovers with all fourteen clubs and all eighteen holes. It is incredibly difficult, yet at the same time, it offers something found in no other sport. To explain, no one but a professional can throw a baseball at ninety-eight mph, or play quarterback in the NFL, or stand a chance in playing basketball against professionals. However, anybody can get lucky (for me, it's usually only once a round) and hit a good golf shot like the professional touring pros. That's both the allure and the frustration.

Making it worse, expectations can exceed abilities if you're coordinated to some degree and not a complete klutz. For others like me, you'll never get to a reasonably mediocre level that you feel you should reach. For most people like that, it's a minor irritation. For me, it is like drinking booze without the fun and a whopper hangover. It's *supposed* to be fun . . . (Don't ask why I continue playing golf. I have no idea.)

I'm not ashamed to admit that golf got to me so badly that one of the first things I thought of when I gave my heart to God was that he could "heal" my game and eliminate the frustration, depression, and anger produced by it. That was in January, the same month in which I came back to God after my long absence. I could barely wait till March with reasonably good weather to test my faith. In fact, I didn't. I headed for the golf course in late February when patches of snow were still in the sand bunkers.

I won't reveal my target score on this first full-scale, all-out application of faith to my golf game as it's not important. Let's just say it's a score I had shot before only a precious few times . . . but wasn't sure I would ever shoot again. And it surely didn't look like I'd reach it again after finishing the front nine five strokes over the scoring pace I needed for a shot at my target. Making up five shots in nine holes for a golfer of my highly limited ability was a stiff challenge. In short, I'd dug myself a hole that would require a truly miraculous final nine holes, a level of golf I'd never played or gotten close to.

Miserable, depressed, and cold on top of it, I stood looking at the course out of the clubhouse window after my miserable half-round of golf, having retreated inside for a hot chocolate. Discouraged, I stood looking

God the Golfing Partner (yes, God!)

out a clubhouse window at leafless trees and an empty course. I remember distinctly saying to myself, "Even God can't help me with my golf game." Ready to pack it in, I felt a gentle urging to go ahead and play the back nine.

The miracle wasn't immediate but building. I didn't hit a hole-in-one nor did I reel off sensational scores on hole after hole. (I never counted strokes until after a round as the golf was usually defeating enough without a running tab of my failure.) What did happen, though, was that as I played along on this cold winter afternoon, I began to experience the presence of God with me. And as I did, a calmness came over me that translated into steady, but certainly not spectacular golf for someone of my experience and ability.

As I played the final few holes, I even began to feel God playing golf through me. (I told you this miracle really requires belief.) On the final hole, after reaching the green, I faced a putt of perhaps forty feet in length or more. And that's no exaggeration or fish-tale. Even professional golfers merely try to get the ball close to the hole on putts of that length. I can't say I even tried to get it close to the hole. The fact of the matter is I didn't even try, period. What I did, because of the incredible presence of God, was to simply say out loud, "Here, Jesus, you putt this one." True story.

Having stepped aside spiritually with my arms as mere tools for the Master—who could master the Masters in Augusta, Georgia—I watched, not with building excitement but as a spectator, the ball roll steadily across the green toward the hole. "Just like it had eyes," as golfers say, the ball plopped into the hole as if it had no other possible place that it could have gone. As God is my holy witness, and indeed he was, the putt evinced no celebration from me. I felt like I had nothing to do with it.

When I totaled my score, I had made up the five strokes from my dismal front-nine performance. More significant, the one long putt that I had allowed Jesus to putt for me meant that by one stroke I had achieved the goal I had set for myself. Jesus, through my hands, surmounted the seemingly insurmountable.

It's difficult to impart the reality of Jesus to me at that moment. Suffice to say, reading my first draft of this essay that I wrote decades ago choked me up with emotion. It was a special moment and time with the Almighty.

Back to who invented golf: The devil didn't create golf as an instrument of evil . . . I don't think. It actually can be fun and even an unforgettable blessing as you've just read.

But what if he did? Genesis 50:20 says God will turn what the devil meant for evil into good, so there!

All I know is that God really does care for all things . . . and that he's an incredible putter.

"I Know God Created Family But Good Grief..."

"Children will be your greatest joy or your greatest heartbreak."
CASSANDRA MILES SNYDER

"You can pick your friends, but you can't pick your family."
MULTITUDES

Breakdown in Aisle 8

As a teenager, my son would put his arm around my shoulders as we would walk around in public. That ranks near the top in blessings for this dad and expresses beyond any words what was in his heart toward me. He never went through that adolescent phase where he was embarrassed to be seen with me.

In his mid-twenties now, he will still throw his arm around my shoulders when we walk anywhere. Could a father ask for anything more? There's nothing more valuable than that beyond another day with him.

I wonder what he was feeling another day in public at the opposite extreme from the joy of just being a son and father together playing golf.

This day was not long after the divorce of his mom and me, and I thought it would be just like any other round of golf we had shared.

The divorce had hit him hard, as it will any child no matter how old or young. Going off to his first year of college didn't mitigate it any, if at all. I learned after the fact he had gotten counseling during his freshman year. Compounding things was a summer job following that year on a literal graveyard crew tending grounds at a cemetery, a job both exhausting and depressing. My happy, carefree, often hysterical son was quiet. A light had dimmed within him, and he was struggling.

As we played golf late that summer on just one more of the many, many times we'd played, I just began to take in, for who knows how many times, how beautiful he is. As a baby and toddler, he'd had silver-dollar size golden curls, freckles across his nose (that his big sisters had names for), milk-white complexion, ice-blue eyes, and somehow the best features of two very handsome grandfathers. As a young man, he's very striking with tousled, reddish-brown hair and the lean hard physique that many young adult baseball players seem to have. Think John F. Kennedy with a beard.

Equal parts love and pity welled up within me for what he had been through with the divorce, and I couldn't take my eyes off him on the course that day.

We stopped at a grocery store afterward and something happened for which I wasn't prepared. Deep, deep sorrow overwhelmed me, and I broke down crying. One of the many great qualities I discovered in him that day is wordless sensitivity. Knowing my Joe, it didn't surprise me, and he saw it coming; he was prepared. Typical for him, he uttered not a word but just held me, my face buried in his chest as I kept repeating, "I'm sorry Joe. I'm so, so sorry" over and over.

I tell anyone thinking of divorce that children, if there are any, will be the real victims. A husband and wife can grow miserable with each other and engage in a staggering death dance better stopped, perhaps, than to continue. I'll grant, as well, that the ugliness of two people painfully dissecting themselves from what was once one body can be worse for children than their parents staying together.

I will also say, though, that in the majority of cases, a husband and wife experience relief. The nightmare of a promising time gone bad after a while will be in the past, and there is both escape and a new world out there with a new life.

For children, though, there is no "what's next" but only the end of "what was." My family was dysfunctional and burdened by an addictive father—me—and stretches of well-hidden lack that, I believe, created a bunker mentality—us alone against the world where everyone around us was affluent. (It's a long story.) It was our world, though, and as a black friend of mine from the deep South explained to me one day about life in a racist environment, no matter how horrible life can be, it's what you've lived and it's all you know.

No offense to my ex-wife and I pray for blessings in her life, but I've never struggled with regrets or sadness. I went on to a new world and life and, in fact, blessings beyond any expectation I could have had. But my children were left with a void where a world and their life used to be. Their memories are of how it ended, not what it was. And again, there's no what's-next with a family that is no more.

The Bible makes an important distinction easily missed, particularly for those who have been divorced. It says God hates divorce, but what he *really* hates is the hardness of heart that leads to divorce. Love can die in a human heart. I've practically begged friends contemplating divorce to persevere in marriage for the sake of children . . . and I've never seen any of them think of this. A dead, cold heart leads into a dead marriage. You can't be partially dead—dead in a marriage, but alive as a member of a family. Divorce is the death of a marriage *and* a family.

I won't fault a husband or wife who, on the surface, don't consider their children, but I've never fallen out of love with a wife or willingly chosen to divorce either time in two previous marriages. I can't judge those who have pursued a divorce.

The few minutes with my son in the grocery, like some seemingly bad things can be, were precious. I thank God for a time when my sorrow not for me but for him could come out. Far more than that, though, I'm thankful for a son who, without shame, embarrassment, or mortification, held his daddy.

This time he put both arms around my shoulders.

Prisons of Presumption

My other book was a "tell-all" in the extreme and to quote Forrest Gump, "that's all I have to say about that." I have another particular piece of tell-all in this book I'm about to share that is harder than any disclosure in my first book, and if you've read that one, you know that is hard to believe.

My wife and I spend a lot of time on the deck of our home talking. We don't own a TV by choice as we see it as a hindrance to communication and togetherness. (Besides, there's nothing on worth watching, except for sports, in my opinion.)

Not to get in my pulpit or on top of my soapbox, but we *want* to talk for the health of our marriage and we even follow a prescribed formula for one weekly conversation to clear the proverbial decks, so to speak. (See "Beating 50 Percent") So far there's been no gunplay or bloodshed, but we've only been married six years at the time of this writing. Both the intent and our prayer are we don't wind up like so many other older couples we see in restaurants who say more to the server ordering from the menu than they do with each other, consumed with their cell phone. That is truly sad.

I was telling my wife one morning I'm tormented at times by my track record in family relationships. I have three children, two of whom—my daughters—have estranged themselves from me.

I have one more estrangement to add to the list and it's tough to do because of fleshly pride and insecurity about you, dear reader, perceiving I am an ogre. (But hey, you've already bought the book so think what you will. Why should I care? Just kidding.)

Prisons of Presumption

Here it is: I went twenty years without speaking to my only sibling, a sister, and the only remaining relative from my immediate family.

I was sharing with my wife this "0-for-3"—two daughters and a sister—and lamenting it, as I'd done countless times. To say my wife has an incisive mind and forthrightness to go with it is understating it. I'd say the Holy Spirit has uniquely gifted her to cut through the clutter and get to the heart of a matter. I've said herein and numerous times that with some things, "the answer is easy, but the solution is hard." Not with my wife. She can give you both an answer *and* an easy solution. On top of that, she can give you the reason making it complicated is stupid. (I could do without that last one but usually get it anyway.)

Her words to me after my lamentation were unforgettable regarding my sister: "Why don't you call her?" She added, with characteristic dismissiveness and a slight touch of exasperation, "You keep people locked in their past." There, in a dozen words, was an answer, a solution, and a lame, illogical, and, yes, stupid reason I maintained estrangement from my sister. What she didn't need to add, but what I got instantly, was everything in a Louisiana nutshell (my wife's home state), plus a revelation: I not only kept my sister imprisoned in her past with estrangement but myself as well.

Before making the call, I reached out first to a lifelong friend who has somehow maintained a close relationship with both my sister and me for the two decades since things went south.

He asked me two questions that were the right test for my reasons for calling besides what my precious wife had given me: What are your expectations? What is your agenda? Great questions to which I could honestly respond "none" and "none." I had no agenda, not even to improve my relationship batting average to a respectable .333 or one-for-three, a number in baseball that will put you in the game's annual All-Star game.

He also said something powerful if not pertinent to reconnection with my sister: "Being right is over-rated." I have trouble remembering who or what is "right" after twenty years, and it's not important. Time and God make that whole issue irrelevant, but it would do well for me to remember this going forward with current and new relationships.

I knew I had changed, working through some major issues. I knew if I had gotten a cold or hostile reception it wouldn't have bothered me. "Oh well" is what I would have thought. I've changed because there was a time, oh twenty years ago, when that would have crushed me. Thank God,

I didn't get that reception, though, as it meant the reunion, reconnection, and reconciliation as God intended.

I see clearly now the danger in over-valuing or over-rating who or what is right and presuming that there's been no change in others and myself. That's a huge presumption, especially if you haven't talked to them in twenty years.

My sister and I had both changed.

The only regret I have is I didn't make the call sooner, but, if I'm not a complete ogre, I know for a fact, I am a slow learner. Maybe it took me twenty years, six years of marriage to a wonderful woman, and no backsliding with God (at least to any major and permanent degree) to make the call.

The restored relationship is marvelous and miraculous with both of us learning things it was important to know. I never knew my mother rejected my sister just as my father rejected me. As a small child, my sister had overheard my mother telling someone she didn't want her during her pregnancy and how she had cried much of the time before my sister's birth.

I learned, too, some things about my mother that indicated at least the possibility of abuse as an adolescent. Those things go very far in explaining the "walls" around my mother I wrote about in another essay in this collection.

My sister feels *wholeness* now, to use her word. We grew up extremely close. For my part, I don't even feel as if there was an interruption in our relationship. We are as close as we ever were.

In short, we've both been set free. I chose to live in a prison of presumption. What I didn't see was that the prison doors I lived behind were never locked. I was always free. And in walking out of that self-imposed prison of silence, I set my sister free as well.

Acceptance and Peace

My late father was a woodcarver and a great one. His mastery was such that it took him to the 1964 New York World's Fair as an exhibitor in the West Virginia Pavilion.

His masterpiece late in his artistic career among dozens of works was a bust of Apostle Paul. At the time of his work on this piece, he was suffering deeply from my mother divorcing him. He suffered, too, in creating it; he told me of throwing it in the trash many times then digging it out to continue working on it. I suspect he struggled with a desire to have the piece express the pain with which he wrestled but finding himself overwhelmed by that pain at times.

The divorce was the last and hardest time in a life filled with pain. Why my mom shared this, I don't know, but she made me aware my paternal grandmother rejected my dad. I would have never known it from how he idolized her. Making it worse, she loved and accepted his five brothers. The divorce was the worst pain he would ever experience, however. My mother was the love of his life and gave him, I'm sure, at least some of the love he had always missed.

His entire life was a desperate striving for recognition and approval. His work with wood brought him both but only mitigated to a degree the damage done.

His Apostle Paul is incredible because it is so subtly expressive, reflecting and blending, somehow, three stories into one inert piece of wood. Deep lines running down Paul's face into a beard are the story of suffering—imprisonments, beatings, shipwrecks—for a mission demanding his all. The second story is in Paul's eyes closed in neither death nor life but in a weary rest after the sacrifice of, again, his all. He had "run his race" and the piece speaks of completion. The piece is mesmerizing not just to the eyes but to the heart and the soul. I never pass it in my home without reflexively looking at it.

The third story is that of my daddy himself. The face is his agony and resignation to loss going beyond losing his wife, my mother. The resignation in the face of Paul differs from acceptance as it is unexpressed utter demoralization. The closed eyes are in wait for death. My dad never got over his and my mother's divorce, and he died within months after my mom. Life was not worth living for him without her in this world even though they had been divorced for eight years.

As his son, I am trying, as we all are, to run my own race. I loved my father, but he *visited* (Deut 5:9 NKJV) upon me, as the Old Testament describes it, the sins of his mother. Perhaps it was inevitable that he repeated with me what she did. He loved me but didn't know how to express it, his mother never having shown him love. This translated, unfortunately, into a rejection of me. To put it as charitably as possible, he kept a seemingly disdainful distance from me. I remember no physical affection from him, no father-son times except for fishing and college football games (and I was a nuisance to him or felt that way), no fun rough-housing, and always a strained silence when we were alone together. I'm sure it was the same with his mother. Without his intending to, he made me feel like something was wrong with me. Ironically, like he with his brothers, I had an older sibling who pretty much was the "golden child" with him. (I discovered much later than I was my mom's golden child and that she had rejected my sister.)

None of us escape suffering in this life and world, but even fewer find acceptance of that suffering and peace beyond it. I consider myself blessed among men as I've experienced suffering but found the peace of God.

Childhood rejection has had a counterpart to my dad's pain of divorce in the last years of his life. I am in my late sixties and have two daughters estranged from me—my oldest daughter from the whole family, my youngest daughter just from me.

Not that it should matter, but anyone who learns of this concludes I was and am a bad father. Chalk it up to human nature, I suppose. We all want to jump to a conclusion. I am guilty as charged to some indeterminate degree, although it is maddening to have people make that judgment without knowing anything about my family or me. (Heck, *I* don't know the degree to which I was a bad father.) I adored my girls but had a closet

Acceptance and Peace

addiction that manifested openly in a very common "twin brother" to the substance to which I was addicted: anger. It was there for my girls to see but never directed at them.

I equate time as an addict and rage to Paul's guilt in persecuting early Christians and my dad's rejection of me when I was a kid. Paul turned to God on the road to Damascus and my dad, who knew God, finally accepted me when I was an adult.

I turned to recovery, but more accurately, the God of recovery and Lord of all to find my own road to Damascus. I found my recognition and approval in God and, to a minuscule degree compared to Apostle Paul, a recovery ministry to help others. It became my mission field, my purpose, and my passion. It also gave me something probably more valuable than anything: peace that has come through acceptance of "things I cannot change," to borrow from the familiar Serenity Prayer.

Acceptance is a silent, immeasurable process with no beginning you can point to or certainty that it is complete. I experience no high emotion about the situations with my daughters like I used to nor does judgment and presumption by others bother me. I will even confess that I forget to pray for my daughters and their husbands. God has blessed me with a wonderful wife and a retirement in my near future I could not have imagined. God truly has blessed "exceedingly abundantly above all that we ask or think" (Eph 3:20 NKJV).

Are my daughters prodigals? I hope so. But if not, that's ok. They are adults. God's love allows us to be free agents and I have to take my cue from him.

In the Bible story, the Prodigal's father is a type for God. I can have open arms and would run to my daughters were they to return to a relationship with me. But my past is not that of a perfect father, nor, do I imagine, was the father who ran to his long-lost son.

We will have our suffering, but there is a mission for me as a follower of Jesus. Paul had his days as a persecutor. My father had his inner demons driving him away from fatherhood. And I, too, have struggled with my own demons.

God says he supplies all our *needs*, not our *wants*. While I want a relationship with my daughters, I have, in him, the peace that I need.

Amen.

My Son the Winner

A friend of mine used to say no parent, whatever the social class, lowliness of their circumstances or education, looks at their newborn and thinks, "Hey, they could grow up to be the manager at . . . " (fill in the name of your favorite fast-food restaurant). Every parent has high aspirations for their children.

Athletics are the great equalizer with social classes. The blue-collar worker may not be able to tell you the location of Yale University, but he knows his son, as a professional athlete, can make more money than any Yale graduate.

I was, as the father of a very athletic son, no different from most other fathers. Every jump shot on his backyard hoop boded at least a four-year scholarship to a college if not a professional career; every swing of his youth-size aluminum bat was the groove for future adult exploits in stadiums across the country; every swing of his cut-down golf clubs put him one step closer to Sunday afternoon stardom in professional golf tournaments.

In his case, a surprisingly fluid golf swing, while still not two years old, believe it or not, fueled expectations and aspirations. Curiously, he would stop playing with any toy as a toddler to watch highlights from any golf tournament on the sports channel, mesmerized for the few minutes it took to replay the highlights before going back to his toy when they were over. Rocket fuel replaced high octane when my son, at age six and the youngest competitor, was one of the long-drive winners in a citywide golf-skills competition.

For not just me, but practically every parent, expectations, aspirations, and ambitions do not lessen but increase as the child grows older. The result, too often, is parents going over an invisible line to become a "Little League Dad" or "Stage Mom" who screams at coaches, teachers, and children alike.

Somehow, in some perverse and tormenting way, success on a baseball diamond or a golf course for a child becomes the salve and balm for the parent's experiences of failure in their own life. They want to live their life through that child, and all too often take that life over and wreck it.

Two years after my son was one of the winners in the long-drive competition, he lost in the same event. It crushed me. As for my son, Joe, his only concern about losing was not that he hadn't done his best, or wasn't as good as the other kids, but that he had let his dad down.

As frustrating as the results were, the attitudes and actions of many of the child golfers were worse. Kids dressing like miniature touring pros arrogantly and flagrantly disobeyed rules before the competition. And unlike adult pros, there was, during actual play, trash-talking and put-downs from some of them, all designed to psyche out and defeat any competitor who would listen. Win at all costs. Get any edge you can. Win for dad or mom.

Walking to the car after the competition, neither Joe nor I quite knew what to say to each other. His concern for my disappointment was proof positive I had crossed over the line into Little League Dad, a jerk. Ego, ambition, and expectations had robbed us all of something that should have been fun.

Loading my son's golf clubs into the trunk of the car, Joe saw a kid who had been a winner also loading his bag in a car behind ours. With no prompting from me, but with a definite prompt from a greater one living within him, my son wished the kid good luck in the regional competition that winners would move onto. The mother of this child stared at Joe as if he'd just landed from Mars, and then managed, after a brief instant of speechlessness, a "thank you" for the best wishes and a stunned, "That's awfully nice of you to say that."

In one brief moment, with just a few words, my son became the winner that day, and I could see instantly the worthlessness of a trophy against the value of a heart where God lives. Somehow, in some invisible and uplifting way, the many lessons from Sunday School, the lessons about a perfect son, and a life given over to a heavenly Father became manifest.

The Son of God did everything right, yet the multitudes that surrounded his place of earthly death surely looked upon him as a loser, an imposter whose ability to perform miracles had run out before he could save himself from the horrid crucifixion reserved for the lowest criminal.

It has always amazed me that even in the agony of dying he promised the believing thief on the cross next to his that "'today you will be with Me in Paradise'" (Luke 23:43 CSB).

Real winning isn't about trophies, the top of a leader board, statistics in a box score, and being the object of admiration and idolization. It is, as my son taught me, about humility, and taking a moment to step outside of one's self to think about someone else, and to express something positive to him or her. My aspirations and ambitions for my son are not that he would be the "winner" but that he would, as another son did two thousand years ago, choose to do the right thing and step outside himself for someone else.

I suspect he's already on his way.

Against the Wind

I used to hear have people say they love their grandchildren more than their children and think they were lying, weird, or both . . . until I had grandchildren. And they're not even technically mine. I inherited them from my wife, two little girls five and seven years old. I'll stop here before I go into grandparent stories. All I'll say is, I should have a t-shirt with "*Don't Ask Me About My Grandchildren*" on the front and "*I'll Bore You to Death*" on the back.

There's an old joke that the reason grandparents and grandchildren get along so well is because they have a mutual enemy. My children are not enemies, as far as I'm concerned anyway, but I would hate to hear their response if you asked them about me. My two daughters estranged themselves from me, as you will have read elsewhere in this collection. I *really* don't want you to ask me about my children. A divorce and their experience of growing up in a dysfunctional home for them were far worse than I ever imagined, apparently. It is my life's tragedy and heartbreak.

The last phase of grief—acceptance—has, I guess, come. I do not grieve anymore and have lost myself in God's manifold blessings with a wonderful wife of six years. (And did I mention two little beautiful granddaughters?!)

I will say I found myself saying something aloud to my wife that shocked me recently, that I wished I had never had children. True confession. As my wife will say, "Children will be your greatest blessing and your greatest heartaches." Making the thought especially shocking was that it put me among a majority of parents who expressed the same sentiment in a survey a newspaper advice columnist took more than forty years ago—70 percent of other parents at the time felt that way. One can only imagine what that percentage might be today.

An important qualifier to the survey, however, is those parents surveyed were anywhere from fifty to eighty years old. I would have never said this when my children were growing up. But that was then, this is now, and I am in my sixties.

I also don't really mean it when I say I wish I had never had them.

The opposite, unfortunately (*very* unfortunately), was my poor dad would have wished he hadn't me when he was a young man. My mom and dad never hid from me that I was an accident. Yes, I know, that sounds horrible, but they didn't know any better than to share that with me. They also told me this, maybe, because there was an addendum: My parents were on the way to divorce when my mother conceived and my dad always viewed me as a Godsend to save their marriage.

The problem was, while he believed this, he didn't act like it. He wasn't the greatest of fathers, to put it mildly, a deeply wounded alcoholic who, like a lot of alcoholic fathers, wounded me, his only son. It took decades to grow God's grace in my heart for my late dad, but grow it has. He was trying to be a father with both hands tied behind his back, a victim of rejection in his own right. His whole life is in the title of an old Bob Seger song, "Against the Wind." A moment I'll never forget was driving to plan his funeral and that song coming on the radio. This poor, poor man's life was against the wind.

Such was our relationship that when I had my son, I would consciously think in every situation daily what my dad would have done and then I would do the opposite. If I was bone tired and Joe wanted to play catch, we played catch. Whatever it was, if I thought my dad wouldn't have done it, I did it. I don't remember my dad ever hugging me or any play time. I also never heard "I love you" except once when I think he felt he had to say it. It had burst from his mouth to my sister while I happened to be standing there. Yet, I know he did love me. He just didn't know how to express it.

I know there was never a day I didn't hug or kiss my son or tell him I loved him.

To be fair and to give glory to God, my father and I grew close after college—the opposite of what has happened with my children. Something changed with my dad or with me.

There was something seemingly insignificant at the time that marked the change. Walking off a golf course after a round with my lifelong friend and my brother-in-law—two of my favorite people on earth—there stood my dad. It's a favorite but flawed memory of him. I walked up to him and did something I'd never done: I hugged him. He was drunk, but it didn't matter then and never did afterward. From that time on, whenever I saw him, he would reach out his arms for a hug.

That didn't make up for the damage done to me as a kid. You can't unscramble eggs, as they say. All he and I both had was that moment and the balance of his time on this earth. And, as with my children and the change in my relationship with them, that was then, this is now.

The "now" was going over to his home weekly to visit him, drawn by something I was unaware of at the time. The annoyance, the thinly veiled disappointment toward me, and the "restless, irritable and discontented" state of an alcoholic were gone. We shared Civil War history, sports, and the most precious thing: time. We also shared love for a baby girl he fathered very late in life in a second marriage. I'll never know why, but when I came to the hospital shortly after her birth to look at her through the window of the nursery, I glanced over at him next to me and he was crying. Only God knows why my presence and acceptance of my new sister touched him.

I expect to be looking through a nursery window again when another grandchild, the first from one of my children, is born.

I'm excited enough to already have bought a onesie with the logo of his dad's, my son's, favorite college team.

As my son gets ready to become a father, I have one bit of advice for him: don't model how you love the little guy as I loved you, even though, I believe, we had a good, good relationship. Instead, love him as God loves us.

I write elsewhere in this collection of my prayer closet and prayer that always begins with "Good morning, daddy God." In my flesh and blood, the knowledge that God is my real daddy rings hollow. I'm flesh and spirit, mostly flesh.

I know he is my daddy, just not in the way that I missed as a kid with my earthly father. It is God's grace that has me continue to love my children with arms always open no matter how far or long they stay away. It is his heart that had me, unconsciously, forgive my dad, be a son to him, and find blessings from him in his last years. It has been his love that has given me a new life with a tremendous wife. In short, he has given me things no earthly father could have.

And did I mention my two granddaughters?

Loving God More than Family

My oldest daughter, Anna, found what I call "her voice" at around sixteen. That is, she began weighing in on matters large and *not* small as you'll read. I'd explain it as a forthrightness and honesty that is unique to her.

One of many examples comes to mind: she very accurately and astutely pointed out to her mom and me that we weren't happy in a church we were attending. Now that was a biggee. Separating from a church we had been in for over a decade and in which we were part of leadership was not something to take lightly. Yet, Anna was a lot like the old advertising campaign for the brokerage firm, E.F. Hutton: "When Anna speaks, we listen." My wife and I prayed about it, although the truth of what Anna spoke registered instantly in our hearts. Shortly thereafter, we moved to another church and I found a men's ministry that did more than change my life: it *saved* it.

She also had no filter between what she was thinking and speaking. Often, she would voice what I and everyone else was thinking but were too afraid or uncertain to say. One day at our new church the pastor casually mentioned that "of course, we all love God more than we do our families." I immediately thought I couldn't say that for myself. Leave it to Anna to bring it up at lunch after church and saying what none of us couldn't or wouldn't: She *didn't* love God more than her family.

That thought did not necessarily trouble me as it did give me something to ponder for probably a full year and a half. And it became more than something to ponder. I couldn't escape it. I imagine I was *supposed* to love God more than my family, but to be honest, I didn't. God helped me along with the spiritual quandary with the still, small voice of the Holy Spirit telling me to stop worrying about it. I just needed to focus on the fact God loved me. (Uh, thank you, God, I guess . . .)

I should add that the whole question or issue led to a deep study of the Bible. I discovered a teacher whose approach to scripture and doctrine, such as it is, was what I had been looking for my entire Christian walk.

Just the other day I heard a man, who I trust implicitly, saying that he and his wife love God more than they do each other. That didn't send me back to Square One, or at least I don't think it did. But it might have because within hours I heard that same still, small voice speak something to me akin to what he first spoke to me about who I loved most. Like the first, it didn't get me past the issue of loving my family before God, but it moved me forward.

Here's the blunt truth about family and it reinforces where one's priority needs to be. Family members might leave you and not just through death. I've chronicled in this book very serious, crushing issues with children—bone of my bone and flesh of my flesh. I've had a marriage of twenty-nine years break apart pretty much overnight. My sister and I didn't speak for close to twenty years. (But thanks be to God, we reunited.)

Jesus isn't going to die a second death. He's not going to divorce me. And he's not going to be in the middle of an offense or resentment that causes him to separate from me.

It comes down to the question we all must answer: "Who is Jesus?" This is the single most powerful and important question each person on this earth must answer, and we all will answer it.

I cut myself a little slack these days on the whole question of who is tops on my love list. Loving someone I've never seen has its problems. But loving someone who I can see has its share of problems too.

My family now, for all intents and purposes, is my wife. I have three adult children sort of. (It's a long story covered elsewhere in this book.) I also have two stepsons and some grandchildren through them that are as much mine as they are my wife's.

Back to my wife: I adore Cassie and know she is God's greatest gift to me. But I had the realization that while I love her deeply, I could live without her if she dies before me. Jesus? Not a chance. Acts 17:28 (CSB) says "For in him we live, and move, and have our being . . . "

Again, if she dies, (and my wife and I are both past age sixty-five) then I still have Jesus. If *he* would die (which he isn't going to do and did already, once and for all), then I have nothing.

If needing Jesus more than anyone qualifies as loving him more deeply than anyone else, then most assuredly I do.

Mame's Walls

I adored my mother like no other son, but I honestly cannot recall having a serious conversation with her. Love was just *there* and very real.

As a teenage boy, at an age when kids are embarrassed by their parents and want distance, I would daily have to hold her and not just for a quick hug. I don't remember us talking; we just held each other, and I'd kiss her cheeks. I loved even her name, Mamie, so much that I stopped calling her "Mom" or "Mother," as I grew older, but "Mame" out of deep, deep affection for her. What I felt for her got into the ridiculous as there were times when I'd ask her to let me put my ear next to her cheek to hear her chew something. Don't ask me why. I just couldn't get enough of a mother who was stoic and most of the time in her own world.

Not that she didn't have her moments. She had a good sense of humor and one of my favorite memories of her was watching a comedian on TV do a stretch that was pretty obscene and initially embarrassing to me in front of my mother but funny, nonetheless. She laughed so hard it wiped out any discomfort I had watching it with her. I laughed at her as much as at the comedian.

I can't define the bond between us because, again, words didn't create it. I'll never forget looking back at her on a sidewalk outside my dormitory as she and my dad left me at college, a full fourteen hours' drive from home. She had more than a sad look on her face but a pained, stricken one. I was to see that same look years later. I guess I gave her something she got from no one else in her life.

Returning home from dropping me off, she cried from Columbia, Missouri to Indianapolis, about a six-hour drive. My dad marveled at how she could cry that much that day, putting a humorous spin on it as he did with a lot of things. When I got married a few years after graduating, she cried for days afterward, knowing in her heart I had made a mistake. That time it wasn't funny; her family (my mom and dad were divorced by that time) thought they might have to have her hospitalized. She was right about the marriage, by the way.

I don't think I or anyone else, for that matter, ever knew what she was thinking, and the fact she didn't share it probably led, in large part, to what she would do later. She began to do something puzzling with greeting cards I noticed immediately that seems small but signaled what was to come: Instead of "Love Mame" it was "Love, *love* Mame." Looking back, I know she had begun a long goodbye a full two years before a final one.

She committed suicide, sitting down on the floor next to the dining room table in her home, putting a pistol to her chest, and pulling the trigger.

She was alone, of course, but then she was always alone, especially in the last chapters of her life. She had married a physically abusive man, living in her own private hell to replace another one of dimensions no one knew.

There are lots of things of which I am ashamed, but what tops the list is what I told my boss at work when he asked how she'd died. I told him she'd had a heart attack. I was ashamed of what she did but not nearly as ashamed as I am for lying.

I don't know about others, but for me, a death by suicide is difficult if not impossible to grieve. You can understand a disease, car wrecks, etc., but you cannot understand despair and depression taking you to that.

I refused to look at her in an open casket at the funeral home, as I wanted no memory of her dead. I always have to find some kind of humor in everything; in this case, I joked later that I may have caused the hinges on her coffin lid to wear out to accommodate the opening and closing to spare me seeing her. I was angrily insistent on this, and my dad and sister honored this. Somebody who put his ear to another's cheek to hear them eat could not look at that face cold and dead.

These essays are to provide a prism on God that I hope can be a blessing, and I don't know how this one fits, dear reader. I do know doctrines of men and denominations are beyond feeble in application to death by suicide. It's folly. It is strictly a matter between God and his child who ended their life.

Mame's Walls

Mame was "his child" and, sadly, she belonged to no one else. Her family of origin kept her at arm's length, and the length of a bottle of gin put an even greater distance between her and my father. He loved her as best he could, but alcohol was his first love.

While she belonged only to God, I belonged to her and had her whole heart. What I didn't have and couldn't have was her mind. I've battled depression and even thoughts of suicide many times, but her pain and my pain are singular and solitary wars fought through separate lives. My pain, I can say *without* certainty, will not overwhelm me but who knows. I am my mother's son and I've often thought I've inherited from her a propensity for depression.

I cringe at including the scripture passage below. It sounds like I'm putting out a doctrine of my own or defending what she did. I'm not. I am, however, writing truth and this reality: while she was physically alone when she killed herself, she was not spiritually alone. There was a grieving Father in love and loving her the same way he did a son 2,000 years ago.

> *"'Can a woman forget her nursing child, or lack compassion for the child of her womb? Even if these forget, yet I will not forget you. Look, I have inscribed you on the palms of my hands; your walls are continually before me.'" (Isa 49:15-16 CSB)*

Mame's walls are no longer before him.

An Imperfect Person But "Perfect Gift"

"Every good gift and every perfect gift is from above, coming down from the Father of lights..."

JAS 1:17 (CSB)

"He who finds a wife finds a good thing."

PROV 18:22 (NKJV)

Bottled Tears

I had a great takeaway from an excellent divorce workshop I attended: don't date anyone for at least a year after your divorce. You need time to heal, time to get comfortable in your own skin, time to know yourself.

Of course, there was a further guideline that every four years of marriage should mean one year you wait to remarry. As a sixty-two-year-old at the time, having been married twenty-nine years, this meant roughly seven years when I'd be sixty-nine or seventy before I should re-marry. Notice I mentioned one great takeaway only. I re-married three years after my divorce and without a walker to get me down the aisle.

Looking back on it, I know why people can't resist dating almost immediately after a divorce and it's simple: loneliness. I'm challenged as a writer to describe its depths for me but will try.

A couple of weeks after my ex-wife moved out from our home, I remember leaving a movie theatre by myself and it felt like I was physically wearing a manhole cover for a necklace. I wanted to collapse and sink into the parking lot pavement. The loneliness was that heavy. And it was inescapable.

I would go out to eat alone and bring a book to read to combat loneliness. I see myself in my mind's eye and think how pathetic that was. It saddens me always to see an elderly man or woman eating alone in a restaurant, knowing they are probably widowed.

What I'll call "unfortunate dating"—something I experienced in spades—provided only respites from loneliness. To explain, I was successful in getting dates and starting relationships, *un*successful in dates and relationships with the right people. As a friend of mine told me, I was operating with a broken "picker." Oh, let me count the ways: a very sad alcoholic (written about elsewhere in this collection); a very precious lady who, when things terminated, told me she was a rape victim, (which explained everything about our relationship or lack thereof); and a very attractive woman twenty years younger who, as best as I can figure, maybe had some father issues. (That one still baffles me.)

Interspersed were some "one-offs," the most memorable of which was a brunch date with a woman that I thought went swimmingly. When I called for the second date, she told me in no uncertain terms that I was all wet. There was spindling, folding, and mutilating accompanying a kind of *review* of me, starting with I was a religious flake. It got worse from there. How someone can deduce absolutely everything about you in an hour and a half is ludicrous to the point of comedy, and I laugh about that one to this day.

One other highlight (or lowlight) was the internet dating thing. The one website I used had a box to check, "Would like to meet you." Stupid, flakey me, I thought "would like to meet you" meant, uh, I'd like to meet you. *Au contraire, mon frère.* Not even close. Finally, a woman on the website I never met, by the way, took pity on me and emailed that it meant, essentially, "bat some emails back and forth, and *then* maybe you can meet."

I remarried, again after three years, and wonder if the loneliness would have ever gone away if I had stayed single. The intensity and weight of it, I know, never did disappear or even diminish. Church, ironically, was where it was the worst.

The problem was the size of the church. It is one of America's largest mega-churches with 20,000-plus members. I always thought it was the easiest place to visit because you could come and go, and no one would ever bother you. Very true for a lot of things. It was also, for me, the easiest place to go from seeming peace and tranquility to utter despair and borderline thoughts of suicide in the span of an hour.

It was nobody's fault. Couples, families, and groups of friends surrounded me in a crowd of probably 6,000 at one of the church's three Sunday services. Unlike in a small church where you're going to stand out and regulars feel obligated to greet you, no one has to do that in a mega-church.

If the sensitivity to loneliness had been weekly, I probably wouldn't be writing this. It would strike when I least expected it, maybe once a month or once every six weeks—far enough apart for me to forget each episode and keep returning.

Bottled Tears

The last episode was the worst, going far beyond being lost in the crowd to wondering if I was losing my mind.

There's crying and then there's uncontrollable sobbing. The sadness hit me after getting onto the interstate near the church after one Sunday service. It came out of nowhere and the depth of it was novel. And I didn't think it would stop.

Psalm 56:8 (CSB) says God bottles our tears: "You yourself have recorded my wanderings. Put my tears in your bottle." The scripture always stuck with me long before my divorce and the tears of that day. God had more to bottle when I watched the incredible movie, *The Shack*, and the scene where the Holy Spirit holds a small bottle to the cheek of a character in the movie. God had a few more tears from me to bottle as I watched that scene.

For God to bottle our tears is an incredible promise. He sees our pain, and he goes beyond just remembering them. It's a visual picture that shows love and compassion that can only come from God.

I made it home from church after getting myself together and decided "retail therapy" was what I needed. (Yep, men do it too, at least this one.) To my astonishment, I cried again on the way to a store. Leaving it and driving home, I cried for the third and final time. I seriously began to wonder if I was permanently losing it.

I don't remember anything about the rest of the day, but a day three weeks from then was unforgettable. I met a woman—the only one I did meet on that website, and yes, it took some major "email tennis" before the meeting could happen. Either God was shining a light on her for me or her closeness to God, like Moses, caused her to glow, but she surely did. To this day, almost six years after we married, I tune out, at times, to nothing but how beautiful she is to me. I'll stare at her when she doesn't know it, particularly at family events. Her beauty to me is not just skin deep either. It's her heart and how much she loves our God. I'll never forget standing by the bathroom door one day while she sang along to Christian music on the radio. I cried different tears, tears of joy and gratitude at her love for God. Very simply, I have never loved anyone like I love my wife, and I know that God gave her to me.

I know, looking back, that God bottles those tears of sorrow. He also bottles tears of joy and gratitude. He has filled my bottle full to overflowing.

It Wasn't a Fair Fight

When I met my wife for the first time, I can't say that I was physically attracted to her. Her hair was, um . . . I'll just say a curiosity. She has naturally curly hair and as folks blessed with it are wont to do, she straightened it or tried to. After we were married, she stopped coloring it and fighting the curls. No exaggeration here, but it is routine for perfect strangers to stop her and remark how beautiful her hair is. Silver in front fades into a beautiful, shining, salt-pepper gray in curls and waves that people not only compliment but also insist on touching.

While she wasn't physically attractive to me, at least not then, I marveled at a glow on her face, bad hair and all, when we first met. It was so remarkable I blurted out, "You're so pretty." It was a substitute for "Your face glows," which would have sounded a little strange.

Thinking back on it, I believe it was a kind of glow like that which showed on Moses' face after he'd been to the mountaintop after coming out of Egypt. As we talked for the first time, she told me about her love for Jesus, and I saw that trips and long stays on a spiritual mountaintop with God were the only things that had brought her through an extremely hard life. I saw God's creation, his daughter.

I went home that night and had three words burning in my mind: "daughter of God." That exerted a powerful draw on me. No, she wasn't physically attractive to me, but her heart and the spirit of God within her were. The next morning, I stopped in the parking lot before I got in my car to drive to work, overwhelmed by two thoughts: one, I felt like I didn't have a choice on dating her; and two, I prayed to God if I ever hurt her that he strike me dead and send me to hell. True story. (I later went back to God,

It Wasn't a Fair Fight

by the way, and asked him to forget that part about sending me to hell. He could still strike me dead, though.)

A huge confirmation on whether she was the woman for me came from my two best friends and spiritual brothers. Both came to me separately after meeting her and told me if I let her get away, they'd kill me. Neither could explain why fully. But it had more to do with me than her. According to them, I talked about her differently than other women I had dated. I talked about her heart and Godliness and not her beauty both above the neck and, uh, below it, if you get my drift.

Here's something that occurred to me as I write this essay: I look back at that and I realize I didn't see Cassie blindly as just another pretty face and physically attractive. No, God gave me sight to see her for who and what she was. "I once was blind, but now I see" with this woman, to borrow from "Amazing Grace."

I later struggled mightily with physical attraction for her not far into our dating relationship. As a matter of fact, one of my spiritual brothers told me that I needed to go on and get married to her . . . or he'd kill me. (That seems to be a recurring theme with my best friends.)

As I got to know her (and as she let her hair be curly), I got to see that without a doubt she was the most beautiful woman in the entire world. Rare is the day I don't tell her that from my heart, much to her disbelief and annoyance. I tell her now that the last thing I want to see on this earth before I see the face of Jesus is her face. I routinely stare at my wife and tune out what she is saying (which gets me in trouble a lot) as her beauty often mesmerizes me. I take time, if she falls asleep ahead of me, to look at her face before I turn the light off. I watch her in small groups of people or at family events as she stands out to me, and I can't believe I'm married to her. I simply cannot get over, and never will get over, how beautiful she is. But recognizing that beauty started first with seeing the beauty of her heart and spirit.

God has brought me a long way and brought to me the greatest blessing of my life in Cassie, surpassing even my children from a previous marriage.

We stayed pure in our courtship, which was a major accomplishment. Not controlling physical attraction would have been a betrayal of God and something I'm not sure I could have forgiven myself for. Six years into our marriage, neither one of us has ever been happier. Is restraint during courtship six years ago a factor in our happiness and relationship today? That's something neither of us will ever know for sure. I do know if I can betray

God, how easy is it to betray my wife and the standards I set for myself as a believer?

The indwelling of the Holy Spirit overpowered worldly thoughts and distractions like hair when I met Cassie. I *had* to pursue a relationship with her without any reason other than she was God's daughter. I *had* to vow I'd never hurt her.

Looking back, I realize we take for granted or minimize the Holy Spirit that dwells within us. The same Spirit raised Jesus Christ from the dead. That's the greatest power ever unleashed on this earth. We can bring death to millions with nuclear power, but what kind of power can produce life *after* death? Now there's a thought if there ever was one.

Our flesh constantly wars against the Spirit. I've written an essay elsewhere in this collection that talks about my fleshly struggle with prayer. But sometimes, in a battle between flesh and spirit, it isn't a fair fight. It wasn't a fair fight when I met my wife. Thank you, Holy Spirit, for that light, that glow on her face.

As I've written elsewhere but have to repeat here, light doesn't diminish darkness. It replaces it.

My Heroine on a Harley

My wife is my hero, not for something she did but for what she didn't do.

At age 11, she stuck her thumb out on Interstate 10 in Houston, Texas and put her hand back in her pocket three days later on a street corner in Los Angeles. In between, she shoplifted food at various places along the way because she had no money. She also spent a night in an Arizona jail. The local police were kind enough or uncaring enough to drive her to the city limits the next day so she could continue her way westward. Unbelievable.

She spent the next nine months on L.A. streets dealing drugs on occasion to get by. When finally found by her family, her father had her sent to a juvenile detention center in Los Angeles before flying her home to Texas. Unbelievable. The nine months on L.A. streets were a walk in the park compared to the center. She feared for her health if not her life every moment there.

I won't go into the reasons for her running away. Her home and family life, needless to say, was far more dysfunctional than most. (And that should be quite obvious from a dad who insisted on that detention center.) She forgave her dad for the time in the detention center and all that came before she ran away.

Despite the degree of dysfunction and maybe because of it, my wife is the most forgiving person I know. In fact, she forgives me so quickly and easily for crap I do or say that I wonder if it's real forgiveness or she's shoving stuff down. I think that those who forgive learn its power and never forget it. So far for me, I'll have to take their word for it. I think I have some

Irish in me as I suspect I suffer from "Irish Alzheimer's": I forget everything but the grudges.

Her grace is truly from God as nobody on their own can be that long-suffering with people. I sometimes think she may have inherited some kind of "forgiveness gene." Many of her family members live into their nineties and one even reached one-hundred years old. You can't live that long, I don't believe, without grace given by God for others.

I won't go into either of her two failed marriages—one that was successful for decades before crashing, and another weird one that never really took off. Again, she's forgiven her ex-husbands and I'll just say there was a lot to forgive.

Interspersed was some required therapy that gives new meaning to the old saying that I write about elsewhere in this book—God works in mysterious ways. Her therapy was a Harley-Davidson, a Road King that weighed around 900 pounds. A psychiatrist *prescribed* the bike for her, by the way.

How can a journey down country roads after a workday remedy a journey through a difficult life? Easy. There's no concern on a Harley for anything but a pothole that might be ahead. When that's your biggest problem and not making the rent or mortgage, college tuitions, unhappy marriages, etc. you've got the world by the short hairs. More specifically, it's just you, God, and the wind—in Cassie's case the wind in her face and the wind of the Holy Spirit in her heart. But the ride must end, you say. Yep, but there's the next day when you can get back on and ride. That's what my wife would tell you.

The bike worked so well and was so unusual it had to be from God. That wasn't the only thing, of course. A neighbor had witnessed to my wife and she had accepted Jesus. My wife went "all in," as only she can do, even surviving the inevitable "church hurt" which, if it hasn't happened to you yet, just wait. She didn't begin a "walk" with God but a *run* pursuing him. It continues for her to this day.

Did her ability to forgive prepare her for a marriage to yours truly? Nope. I pray daily to not just my Father in heaven but to my *Father-in-law* in heaven to be a good husband. That gives me a whole different perspective on her and more importantly, how I should treat her. Also, God brought me through some bumps in the road myself, and my wife has gotten the best years of me on this earth. I'm not, however, like fine wine, getting better with age. Not even close.

My Heroine on a Harley

I think I appreciate my wife so much because the bulk of my ministry has been to addicts who've seen and experienced hell on earth as she has.

Why did my wife succeed? First of all, she keeps it simple. It's fair to say she uses the words "choice" and "choices" daily. I've learned to apply those words to my life. Do I take a drink today or not? Do I look at a woman other than my spouse with lust? Do I exercise patience when someone is rude or abusive? It goes on and on, and it's virtually every moment in the course of my day.

Her big choice and why I admire her more than anyone on this earth is again, for what she didn't do. She didn't quit on a God who cannot take back what he did on a cross.

He didn't quit either.

Beating 50 Percent

I tease my wife a lot. Almost without fail, in giving our orders to a waiter or waitress in a restaurant that serves alcohol, I'll ask if she'd like a "big ol' glass of vodka." Except for a rare glass of wine, she's a complete teetotaler.

I haven't ever said this to anyone (and won't), but I've mentioned to her that one of these days I'm going to introduce her as my "third" wife, as in predecessor to a fourth.

I joke, but the statistics for third marriages are no joke at all. Close to 75 percent end in divorce as compared to around 65 percent for second marriages and 50 percent for first marriages.

That's a scary-high percentage of divorce for third marriages and I don't want it to happen to us. My wife says I go about everything, whether it be work or play, "hammer and tongs," and that includes our relationship and marriage. I want our marriage—now past the six-year mark—to work, and I work hard at making sure it does . . . too hard. (More on this later.)

One key, if not *the* key, to a healthy marriage, I believe, is emotional intimacy—no secrets, complete vulnerability, confession, and honesty that can, on occasion, be painful. And I believe in pursuing intimacy . . . even scheduling it (*emotional* intimacy, not the other kind). A tool my wife and I use (a hammer?) is a brief series of questions for weekly discussion that a remarkable young couple, relative newlyweds, developed entitled "Beating 50 Percent." Except for one (and I'll let you guess which one), the questions you ask of each other are pretty easy. Here they are:

1. What brought you joy this week?
2. What was something that was hard?

Beating 50 Percent

3. What's something I can do for you this week?
4. How can I pray for you this week?
5. Is there anything that's gone unsaid, convictions, confessions, unresolved hurt?
6. What's a dream, desire, or thought on the forefront of your mind this week?
7. A question of your choosing.

If you didn't guess number five, you're probably carrying a lot of secrets, are indestructibly invulnerable, or you're as tight-lipped as a wooden Indian. As I've warned the dozens of men to whom I've shared this exercise, number five can take two minutes or two hours.

Far less than discussions of what's "gone unsaid, convictions, confessions, and unresolved hurt" have sent married couples to divorce court, I'm sure.

We've used "50 Percent" for most of our marriage. The questions can be great "catcher-uppers," they open doors to discoveries about each other, and they seem to always lead to resolving issues or disputes if any are on the table.

But wait.

The divorce rate for people in third marriages, again, is close to 75 percent. That's, um, us. We need something more to cover that extra 25 percent chance we'll divorce and for a reason that blindsided me.

A first or second divorce breaks some kind of invisible seal on failure. Whether it's a minor tiff, sparring a few rounds, or going the full fifteen, the first thought is, "Screw it. I failed at this twice. What's another failure?"

It shocked me for a lot of reasons, not the least of which was having no idea this card was in the deck. Marriage is the most important covenant you can make, and why, as a believer in God, would I accept failure so readily? I still don't have the answer to this, but I have the solution, which I'll get to momentarily.

Just recently, I got a revelation that was a spiritual eye-opener, the exact opposite of being blind-sided: the "gone unsaid" and "unresolved hurt" part of number five in "Beating 50 Percent" had led me to score-keeping or keeping a tally in my mind of offenses to load up and fire at my wife weekly. First Corinthians, chapter thirteen—the "love chapter"—is specific about this: Love "does not keep a record of wrongs" (1 Cor 13:5 CSB). In my effort to keep everything out in the open and up-front, I was keeping alive some things that needed to die and die quickly.

Long before I realized I was into record-keeping of offenses, one of my closest friends, who happens to be a counselor, encouraged me to remember something when disagreements arose with my wife: When all is said and done—tiff, tussle, thrown objects—the question I ask of myself is, "Does she love me?" Wow. That puts any offense in the right perspective. So far, by God's grace and her incredible capacity for forgiveness (more on that, too), I can safely say, "yes she does."

If I ask myself that question, offenses and disagreements, and whether the toilet paper roll goes over the top or underneath (it goes over the top, by the way), become minor or aren't worth time and worry.

I've written in another essay that my wife has such an amazing capacity for forgiveness that I used to think she shoved things down. Nobody could forgive that fast and that completely. I've come to realize her forgiveness is real because of something very simple: She doesn't let a moment go by if she's offended before praying. Her forgiveness is almost as fast as switching on a light switch, and what she does is bring God's light into an offense.

Reminding myself that my wife loves me flips another switch within me: grace. No, she's not perfect but as I have said all through our brief marriage, she's perfect for me.

I could be wrong on her not being perfect though. God says "every perfect gift is from above" (Js. 1:17 KJV) and he gave her to me. 'Nuff said.

So, I'll cover that difference between 50 percent and 75 percent with that simple but profound, hugely powerful thought: This woman loves me. I pray that will always be the case in my marriage and in yours too.

A Couple More Random Rants: Dying and Maybe Someone who Should be Dead (?!)

"..."
THE DEAD

"Dead men tell no lies, or anything else, for that matter."
UNKNOWN

Control Freaks and Controlled Freaks

I'd like to add a variation to a common one used in psychology slang: *controlled* freak. I should be on a Mount Rushmore of controlled freaks. Control freaks, of course, control everyone around them. Controlled freaks like me wait on control freaks to destroy them.

Aside from fear and the anxiety that drives you either to control or be controlled, the two types have zero in common. Control freaks say, "never again" when a threat looms in their world. Controlled freaks say in exasperation, "Oh no, not again!" Big difference.

Even though I'm in my sixties, I'm trying to do something about it. Einstein said insanity is doing the same thing over and over expecting a different result, so maybe I'm not completely crazy.

The source or arena for my latest anxiety is a high-stress job, which God dropped out of the clouds into my lap. My experience for the position? A couple of hours of cramming online for the interview and learning a few buzz words. I've never thought of myself as a fiction writer but when I think where resumes have taken me . . .

I also have the willingness (ignorance?) to try anything. That may sound admirable, but that's for hobbies, sports, or food. Work is another matter. I loved the TV advertising campaign built around an unqualified person doing something amazing; "No, I'm not a brain surgeon. But I did stay at a Holiday Inn Express last night." I relate to the person, but I need to *live* in a Holiday Inn Express.

I compensate by willing to learn, even if it is on the fly, and I will try to cover the learning curve with, I'll say, energetic effort. (I can't say "hard work" as that would imply I know how to actually *do* the work.) The trick for me has been to get God's help and not repeat what seems like inevitable mistakes.

It's my luck that my last rodeo, career-wise, would be one where a single mistake can cost my company millions of dollars and, of course, my job. Add to that some very personal politics, attendant in every office, but "steroidal" with two associates, one of whom is (or is supposed to be) a born-again Christian. (Can you say, as this person I know has often said to my boss, "Ken should be fired"?)

I'm not ashamed to admit the stress drove me to two prescription medications, both of which I decided were ineffective. I have stress only a relatively small percentage of the time, so the first prescription may have been ok, but I was taking it during a lull. The second one definitely didn't work, as I not only had anxiety when stress came but depression in its wake—what I call a "trip to the pit."

There's a silver lining to every cloud always and both pit trips and a stressful job have meant for me a more disciplined prayer life. That hasn't been a choice. I have *had* to pray, and God has gotten me out of jam after jam.

Like most, if not all of us, but particularly for a controlled freak, I have no clue what God is doing. I have hope, though. As strange as it may sound to readers who don't struggle with anxiety, that's a giant leap forward. The issue for me is self-reliance with predictable "o-fer" results, to use a baseball metaphor. Think 0-for-1,000.

Realizing that fear is at the root of anxiety is common sense . . . for everyone but a controlled freak. I can see it easily in a control freak that says, "I don't need God. I can handle it myself." For a controlled freak it's more complicated and crazier: "God can't help me, and I can't help me either."

The pride at work for a controlled freak is obvious, at least according to eight "Pride Slides" I discovered online one day. (Coincidence, huh?) It pretty much put the blame for anxiety where it belonged: on me. With someone controlled, it's pride in reverse with, I believe, worse repercussions. Say hello to fear and trembling, catastrophizing everything, self-absorption, life as a perpetual victim, entitlement, weeping and gnashing of teeth, and general misery.

Someone once told me I need self-control. Nope. That's what has gotten me into anxiety in the first place; I've been dependent solely on a "self" that I don't trust along with God or anyone else. Maybe there's another new term that needs to rule, at least, my life: *God*-controlled.

Stage-Fright Stuttering and Miss Spry

Miss Spry, my third-grade teacher at Wilcoe Grade School in Wilcoe, West Virginia was anything but spry. "Sour" is the word that comes to mind, at least that's the best word to describe her expression when she'd call on me to read. It was as if she'd bitten into something extremely sour or I had just crawled out of a swamp or both. All because I stuttered badly when attempting to read aloud before the class.

I didn't stutter more than gag. I could barely get the first syllable out, if that, much less a word. I guess you would call it stage-fright stuttering—actually, performance-anxiety, to use the clinical definition—as I didn't stutter in normal conversation but only when called upon to read.

Miss Spry wanted me kicked out of the school because of this. If you're a parent, you can guess how my parents responded. They paid a visit to the school to have a talk with Miss Spry and the school principal. I have no idea what went on behind the scenes, but I remained at Wilcoe Grade School for the rest of the year.

Just saying here, but I'm not sure the punishment fits the crime. Did she think there was a school I could go to just for kids with my issue?

I remember getting books and reading to myself in our basement. I read like a champ, thinking I was practicing, and that this would do the trick. I want to say somewhere in hell Miss Spry burns when I think of that, but that would be a sin. (Oops, did I just write that . . .)

As you can tell, it's an awful memory that's burned pretty deeply on my brain and worse, very obviously on my soul. How do you get by things like this?

Forty Days

In my case, it's focusing on the fact it *is* in the past. I love reading from a text in a men's group where that's part of the routine. (That's mainly to keep an agonizingly slow reader from getting the task.) I had the lead in a senior class play at my high school. I commandeered a college English class with an impromptu lecture/rant on something or other. Presenting advertising ideas to full board rooms was exciting fun. I've spoken to any number of men's groups in churches. And one of the greatest blessings of my life was speaking to a conference of 500 men.

I only had this performance-anxiety during the third-grade year. God took it away after that.

I think of how Moses had a speech impediment, believed to be stuttering. Because of it, he begs off leading the people when God commands him to. So God says, in so many words, "Fine, Aaron can do the talking for you."

Somewhere along the line, Moses doesn't need Aaron to do his talking. He comes off the mountain after forty days and has plenty to say. In fact, he's got an earful for Aaron who has watched the people build a golden calf.

Maybe Moses still stuttered at that point. Maybe he didn't. On the mountaintop with God, if it was a dialogue (and it probably was), I can imagine God smoothing out his speech. And I'd like to think his stuttering went away totally with the people.

These are questions only folks like me who suffered from stage-fright stuttering or those more unfortunate with chronic, all-the-time stuttering are curious about in the next life in heaven.

One thing is for certain: God didn't let it bother him when it came to choosing Moses to lead his people. He also doesn't let anything bother him when choosing *any* of us to do his will and his works in this world.

I'll never forget a sermon that challenged us to look at the biggest weakness in our lives and recognize that it is a portal to God's strength. "'[F]or My strength is made perfect in weakness'" (2 Cor 12:9 NKJV).

Moses had lots of issues: He was adopted, probably the source of classic rejection issues and anger problems. (Anger problems are stating it mildly. He *killed* an Egyptian he caught abusing two Hebrew slaves.) He may have had organization issues as his father-in-law, Jethro, had to help him set up kind of an executive board to hear all the matters that were coming to him alone. He also had well-documented issues with anger, striking a rock to bring forth water when God told him to speak to it, a mistake that cost him entry into the Promised Land.

Stage-Fright Stuttering and Miss Spry

In short, he was, like everyone in the Bible: very human.

I have no idea why God delivered me from performance-anxiety. He blessed me with the ability to write, I hope, but he also got my speech straightened out. Maybe he knew I was going to have to talk about what I wrote. At any rate, I'm extremely grateful and consider it the first big miracle of my life.

But what if I still had it? Instead of thinking of it as a weakness, God would have given me the strength to compensate for it mightily. Think about how someone blind has additional keenness in other senses.

As for whether it was a miracle or not, consider this from *Psychology Today* addressing the "social anxiety disorder" or fear that can cause stage-fright stuttering: "simple adjustments in cognitive behaviors can help ease that fear—for example, bring notes, don't convince yourself that you will bomb, make eye contact to ease the tension." Tell that to a third-grader. Really? My parents, I know, told God the problem. Problem solved. Thank you, thank you, thank you, Lord God Almighty.

For sixty years, I've never had a problem with stage-fright stuttering. My friends might tell you, though, it's created a new problem . . . for them. They wish I'd shut up.

On Death, Dying, and Dollars

I have a different perspective on death that I think should come from being a believer. I heard someone say that their dad, as he died, seemed to deflate as his spirit left his body. My desire is to close my eyes with my wife's beautiful face before me and open them to see the face of Jesus.

Her perspective on death is as mine but with different terminology. For me, my earthly body is a carcass. My wife calls her's an "earth suit."

We are both in our sixties and we have planned what we want done with our earth suits. (I'll use her better-sounding term.) Two things drive a decision we've made, one of which is that this earthly body is nothing, just a suit we wore. The second is something just plain practical and I believe totally logical: money.

With apologies to Elisabeth Kubler-Ross, author of *On Death and Dying*, I think she missed a sixth stage of grief that may be the most grievous of all: funeral costs.

I'm donating my body to science and it is a bargain extraordinaire: zip, zero, nada. That's for hauling my dead, cold keister off; embalming; and even, ultimately, cremation of what's left of me. The only catch is it could be a month or two years before the medical school students complete slicing and dicing. What's left goes to the crematorium. The only cost would be mailing my ashes to whomever I designate for $25. Of course, my wife or someone else could *haul ash* (I couldn't resist) after swinging by the campus for nothing. Or they could forego that option and just let the university dispose of me at their burial site. (The university has a burial site? Who knew?) If there's a better bargain in America, somebody let me know.

On Death, Dying, and Dollars

The trick is to not suffer a violent death, kill myself, or die from a few infectious diseases, including something called Creutzfeldt-Jakob disease (Mad Cow disease for humans, the longest odds on the board for my ultimate demise). I can't be an organ donor, either. They want the whole package intact or nothing. So, providing I exit this world with a whimper, not a bang, I'm good to go and of value to medical school students.

Of course, we all know the only other group, besides future doctors, that I am of value to dead: the fine folks down at the local mortuary. All for somewhere between $6,000 and $8,000 (the national average) they will be happy to embalm me; perform other bodily preparations whatever they may be (and I don't want to know); dress me; comb my hair, or what's left of it; load me in a casket; haul me off; and adopt faux expressions of sympathy at just the right moments for family and friends.

No thanks.

My wife lost both parents within six months of each other and saw the beauty of her and her brothers taking some time to quietly reminisce shortly after her dad died and just after an ambulance carried his body to the state university's medical school. The contrast with her mother's elaborate, carefully planned "grief-fest" sealed the decision of body donation for my wife.

As for me, I've become either cheap in my old age or someone immensely logical. I suspect a little of both, but I'll let you be the judge.

Actually, I'm not the least bit interested in donating to science. What I am interested in is *not* donating to a funeral home and cemetery.

My aversion to America's "death industry" began when my next-door neighbors I had grown close to died within a year or so of each other. Maybe curiosity registered on my face as to why there was a coffin at Harry "Tubby" Boyle's wake; I thought he was supposed to be cremated? At any rate, his sister, honoring form for an Irish wake, perhaps, sidled up to me at the casket and volunteered, "Tubby ain't in there, ya' know."

Ok, this is a funeral home. The obit was in the paper with all the details. We are in the middle of a wake. And we have a coffin. What are we missing here? Oh yeah, the dead body. Yep, he *was* cremated but somehow the family was talked into casket rental for the wake.

Now that's salesmanship on somebody's part: "Mrs. Boyle, you'll want to rent a casket as it provides an object for your husband that is necessary for the grieving process." No, the object you refer to is for filling with a body. How about we forget renting an empty box and just go with an urn on a table or something?

The same deal applied to Kate Boyle's funeral except she did get some use out of a casket. She, too, went the cremation route but not before spending time in an open casket at her own wake. Her son, this time, provided the comment that stuck with me: "She's just renting the casket. You know how cheap Mom was." (Wonder if they divide caskets between "new" and "demo" models in the showroom?)

The cliché is that funerals are for the living. Yeah, yeah, I get it—family, friends, grief, closure, etc.—but the reality is, we wouldn't have funerals without somebody dead, and in my godfather Tubby's case, we didn't even have that. Empty caskets, rented caskets—funerals are for undertakers.

Call me crazy. Call me a tightwad. But ultimately, whether primped by morticians or carved up by medical students, call me dead. Sure, you can't take it with you, but you can leave it behind in an urn (albeit less than usual, accounting for industrious med students) and in your estate. My hat's off (and everything else, of course, at some point in time) to the university's med school). See you later, or folks down at the school will see me later. I'm getting a new body in heaven and God knows I need one.

Apostle Paul got it *mostly* right in First Corinthians 15:55 (KJV) when he wrote, "O death, where is thy sting?"

True for the dead. Not so much for the survivors and their bank balance.